The Complete

Personal Finance Handbook:

Step-by-Step Instructions to Take Control of Your Financial Future—

With Companion CD-ROM

By
Teri B. Clark

The Complete Personal Finance Handbook: Step-by Step Instructions to Take Control of Your Financial Future: with Companion CD-ROM

Copyright © 2007 Atlantic Publishing Group, Inc.
1405 SW 6th Ave. • Ocala, Florida 34471 • Phone 800-814-1132 • Fax 352-622-1875
Web site: www.atlantic-pub.com • E-mail: sales@atlantic-pub.com
SAN Number: 268-1250

ISBN-13: 978-1-60138-047-0   ISBN-10: 1-60138-047-X

Library of Congress Cataloging-in-Publication Data

Clark, Teri B.
  The complete personal finance handbook: step-by-step instructions to take control of your financial future: with companion CD-ROM / Author: Teri B. Clark.
    p. cm.
Includes bibliographical references and index.
ISBN-13: 978-1-60138-047-0 (alk. paper)
ISBN-10: 1-60138-047-X (alk. paper)
1. Finance, Personal. 2. Investments. I. Title

HG179.C586. 2007
332.024--dc22
                    2007013112

Printed in the United States

Printed on Recycled Paper

We recently lost our beloved pet "Bear," who was not only
our best and dearest friend but also the "Vice President of
Sunshine" here at Atlantic Publishing. He did not receive
a salary but worked tirelessly 24 hours a day to please
his parents. Bear was a rescue dog that turned around
and showered myself, my wife Sherri, his grandparents
Jean, Bob and Nancy and every person and animal he met
(maybe not rabbits) with friendship and love. He made a
lot of people smile every day.

We wanted you to know that a portion of the profits of this
book will be donated to The Humane Society of
the United States.

–Douglas & Sherri Brown

THE HUMANE SOCIETY
OF THE UNITED STATES ©

The human-animal bond is as old as human history. We cherish our animal companions for their unconditional affection and acceptance. We feel a thrill when we glimpse wild creatures in their natural habitat or in our own backyard.

Unfortunately, the human-animal bond has at times been weakened. Humans have exploited some animal species to the point of extinction.

The Humane Society of the United States makes a difference in the lives of animals here at home and worldwide. The HSUS is dedicated to creating a world where our relationship with animals is guided by compassion. We seek a truly humane society in which animals are respected for their intrinsic value, and where the human-animal bond is strong.

Want to help animals? We have plenty of suggestions. Adopt a pet from a local shelter, join The Humane Society and be a part of our work to help companion animals and wildlife. You will be funding our educational, legislative, investigative and outreach projects in the U.S. and across the globe.

Or perhaps you'd like to make a memorial donation in honor of a pet, friend or relative? You can through our Kindred Spirits program. And if you'd like to contribute in a more structured way, our Planned Giving Office has suggestions about estate planning, annuities, and even gifts of stock that avoid capital gains taxes.

Maybe you have land that you would like to preserve as a lasting habitat for wildlife. Our Wildlife Land Trust can help you. Perhaps the land you want to share is a backyard—that's enough. Our Urban Wildlife Sanctuary Program will show you how to create a habitat for your wild neighbors.

So you see, it's easy to help animals. And The HSUS is here to help.

The Humane Society of the United States
2100 L Street NW
Washington, DC 20037
202-452-1100
www.hsus.org

TABLE OF
CONTENTS

CHAPTER 2: Understanding Banking 37

CHAPTER 3: Why Save And How 47

CHAPTER 4: The Habit of Saving And Starting Early 63

CHAPTER 9: Avoiding Debt and Bankruptcy 117

CHAPTER 10: Fixing Your Credit 127

CHAPTER 14: Avoiding Investment Scams   183

CHAPTER 15: Creating Fixed Income   201

CHAPTER 16: Taxes — What You Should Know   211

FOREWORD

By Juan Ciscomani

As a trainer of financial counselors, I have witnessed the average consumer's pitfalls firsthand. I understand the mistakes that can be, and often are, made. I also know the steps to take to prevent a financial disaster and how to recover from one that has already occurred.

So many consumers believe that financial management is about denying themselves life's pleasures. They do not see that financial management is simply managing their money in a way that leaves them in control; it is about tempering wants with reality.

Will you ever have debt? For most of us, the answer is yes.

Debt is not a bad thing if you understand what you are doing before you get yourself caught up in the world of "big, fast, and beautiful." Whipping out the credit card and then cringing over the bill and the interest charged is not control. The point of money management is to make conscious decisions and to control your money — not letting your money control you.

If you already are in financial trouble, there is no one right way to fix the problem. It would be great if there were a quick fix, but it took time to get into trouble and it will take time to get out of it. You have to look at the root cause. Over-spending habits will require a different fix than late payment habits. Not only will changing poor habits take time, but cleaning up the credit mess reflected in your credit score will take time as well.

Having said that, there is hope.

If you are just starting out, reading this book will give you choices concerning your present and your future. If you are financially sound but do not know how to move toward savings and retirement, you will find the answers as you peruse these chapters. Finally, if you are in financial trouble, this book can help you find a way out and create a better financial path.

Knowledge is key in all things. *The Complete Personal Finance Handbook* will give you the knowledge you need for a better financial future.

Juan Ciscomani
Senior Instructional Specialist
Credit-Wise Cats
Take Charge America Institute for
Consumer Financial Education and Research

John and Doris Norton School of Family and Consumer Sciences
The University of Arizona
Phone: 520-626-5376
Fax: 520-621-3209
http://tcainstitute.org/

Juan Ciscomani began to develop his expertise in personal finance throughout his academic career at The University of Arizona. Joining the Credit-Wise Cats (named after the University of Arizona's Wildcats) allowed him to become a highly trained counselor and offer personal, financial education to University of Arizona students, faculty, and the greater Tucson community. In addition, Ciscomani developed a wide variety of Spanish language money management workshops to cater to the needs of the Hispanic population in Tucson. Moreover, through the Credit-Wise Cats and Students in Free Enterprise (SIFE), Ciscomani participated in regional and national case study competitions and other creative programs with the sole mission of teaching personal finance. In May of 2005, Ciscomani graduated Cum Laude with a Bachelor's degree in political science from the University of Arizona.

Upon graduation, he was one of twenty recently graduated Hispanic scholars in the United States selected to participate in the Congressional Hispanic Caucus Institute (CHCI) Public Policy Fellowship Program in Washington, DC. During his nine-month fellowship, Ciscomani worked as a Legislative Assistant in the House of Representatives for Rep. Loretta Sanchez of California. In this position, he researched, tracked, and developed legislative initiatives and appropriations requests in issue areas, including: financial literacy, education, housing, telecommunications, and environment. He also handled all small business, economic development, and banking issues for Representative Sanchez.

After completing the CHCI Public Policy Fellowship Program, Ciscomani returned to Arizona and rejoined the Credit-Wise Cats and SIFE team at the University of Arizona. As Senior Instructional Specialist, he now trains the Credit-Wise Cats and assists them in developing personal finance knowledge in a broad spectrum of topics. Furthermore, Ciscomani researches and writes personal finance case studies with solutions that are used at college level personal finance case competitions and regional and national personal finance case study competitions. During the past year, Ciscomani played an integral role in launching and coordinating the Xtreme Xplorations program at a new local charter school, Wildcat Middle School. As program manager, he teaches personal finance to the students, in addition to training, supervising, and coordinating university students and volunteers on a weekly basis.

Ciscomani's decision to return to Tucson was primarily based on his interest in contributing to his community. Within the past year, he helped initiate the Pima Community College Alumni Association and currently holds a position on the new Alumni Board. As a result of his involvement with the Alumni Association, he also sits on the Pima Community College Foundation Board of Directors.

CHAPTER 1:
Budgeting

What Is a Budget and Why the Need for One?

DEFINITION:	A budget is simply a game plan for managing income to cover the cost of living over a set period of time.

The best way to start taking control of personal finances is with a monthly budget. It can be complex: walking around with a notepad and pen itemizing every purchase down to a single pack of gum, or it can be a simple list of general categories: rent, utilities, transportation, and entertainment.

Creating a budget provides knowledge of:

- Monthly expenditures — the money going out.

- Monthly income — the money coming in to cover expenditures.

First Step to Financial Success

Personal financial planning consists of three general activities:

- **Controlling day-to-day finances** for freedom to do necessary and recreational activities. Controlling these finances promotes a sense of financial security.

- **Choosing a course of action** for short- and long-term financial goals. Short-term goals include purchasing needed appliances for the home or finding reliable transportation. Long-term goals include buying a house, sending children to college, and retiring comfortably.

- **Building a financial safety net** will help avoid financial disasters, such as unemployment, poor health, or personal tragedy by saving enough money to cover all expenses for at least three months; saving for six months will increase safety net security.

Financial planning works for those who make thousands of dollars a year and those who make hundreds of thousands of dollars a year. All fiscal stations of society need a budget. Purchasing power determines credit line; being over extended is not just a problem with the poor. A budget is the first step toward financial success.

Habits Consume Money

Years ago, I believed that I knew where my money went. I felt certain that I was keeping track and that I was on course. However, I took a challenge that I would like to propose:

Keep track of every cent spent for one month. Carry a notebook and jot everything down—everything. The outcome will be shocking. Quite a bit of money is lost to small expenditures — money that could add up to big savings.

Those eat-out lunches instead of something from home, those extras in the shopping cart, and those certain habits that cost more than realized can all be pared. Start by examining all areas of the monthly budget.

Here is a look at the entertainment budget with a savings option. Going to the movies twice a month with a spouse or a friend will cost $40. By opting to become a member in a $10-a-month video-by-mail program, the savings equal $30 a month. Thirty dollars over the course of a year is $360, and over the course of 10 years, if this money is put into a savings account, $4,000.

Smoking! Quitting a $30 a week habit saves $120 a month. Putting this money into a savings account yields almost $18,000 after 10 years.

Here are a few others:

HABIT	YEARLY COST
Daily Cup of Coffee	$547/yr
1 Hardback & 3 Paperback Books/Mo.	$690/yr
Lunch Take-out 5 days/wk @ $5-$10/day	$1300 - $2600/yr
3 Drinks at a Bar/Wk.	$936 - $1092/yr
3 Six-packs of Beer/Wk.	$624 - $936/yr

Tracking expenses shows the flow of money, helping create a budget that allows for the fun things, while reaching short- and long-term financial goals.

The Components of a Budget

Income

Salaried earners have fixed monthly incomes. Income for hourly earners fluctuates due to decreased hours or overtime. Commissioned and self-employed earners' income fluctuates even more.

Salaried earners simply enter into the budget what is brought home each month. Hourly earners list the pay for the typical number of hours worked. If overtime is only worked in November and December, do not include overtime as part of salary. If only 35 hours a week are worked, instead of 40, for a majority of the year use the 35 hours as a basis for the budget.

Commissioned and self-employed income is harder to judge, especially if the workers are new to the job. After working three or four months, average income will be easier to judge. For the purposes of a budget, it is much better to figure a lower number here and be surprised at the end of the month with more money rather than a lack of it.

Fixed Bills

After finding income, it is time to look at outgoing money. The first place to look is at fixed bills.

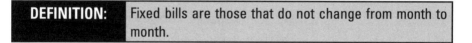

DEFINITION: Fixed bills are those that do not change from month to month.

One of the major fixed bills is rent or mortgage payment, but they also include monthly car payments, and insurance, such as medical, life, auto, renters or mortgage.

Savings is the one fixed expense that most people ignore. To get finances in order, it is necessary to save every month. Savings need to come right off the top. For most people, $50 to $150 per week works well. However, even $10 a week to get into the habit of saving is better than nothing.

Variable Bills

DEFINITION: Variable bills do not stay the same from month to month because of how the product is used or the service changes each month.

Fluctuating monthly bills are called variable expenses. They include electricity, water, natural gas, and oil, credit card bills, gasoline, and groceries. Determine an average monthly cost for each.

To find out how much to budget for electricity, take the average of the last six to twelve months.

Electric bills are usually higher in the summer and winter than in the spring and fall. Averaging during high billing months allows you to estimate high and provides you with a buffer in case of above average costs.

Ideally, credit card bills and car payments will be zero each month.

Discretionary Funds

DEFINITION: Discretionary funds are money that can be spent freely and without guilt.

After income, savings, fixed bills, and variable bills come discretionary funds (mad money) spent for pizza with friends, those to-die-for new shoes, tickets to a ballgame – those things you can live without. They are the reason you need a budget—to show how much money is left to enjoy after bills are paid.

A budget also helps make choices. A less expensive apartment and a less expensive car mean having more money to spend for fun or to invest. A budget does not have to be a straitjacket—it is a game plan that uses a top-down model. Take care of the important things first, and then allocate the remainder.

Analyzing Your Budget

Being aware of spending habits and changing them will result in a surprising amount of savings. Examples of common areas of budgetary abuse include eating out, taking taxis instead of mass transit, and buying anything you do not need or will not use. Changing these habits takes discipline but does not mean deprivation. Some examples might be purchasing fewer magazines or CDs, using the library instead of buying books, or waiting to rent videos of the movies rather than going to movie theaters.

CASE STUDY: DIANE PEARSON

People who do not put aside money tend to think they are not vulnerable to financial losses, and they often make financial mistakes that will cost them in the future. To avoid such mistakes, think about the following:

Set up an emergency reserve account. This money needs to be set aside and it needs to be liquid (available immediately with no withdrawal penalty). It should be used

CASE STUDY: DIANE PEARSON

if you are unable to work, out of work, or if an unexpected expense arises, such as a transmission or a new furnace.

Get personal disability insurance. Group insurance through your employer is not enough because it does not move with you when you change jobs. Statistics show that young people will go through three different jobs in the first ten years of employment. Additionally, when the unemployment insurance is paid out to you via your employer, it is considered taxable income. Personal disability insurance is not taxable.

Participate in an employer-provided retirement plan, especially when you, the employee, match all or some part of the funds. Put in at least as much as they will match. If they match 25 percent of each dollar up to 3 percent of your annual income, you should put a minimum of 3 percent of your annual income into the plan. Even if you leave the job, this plan will still be available to you and can be rolled into another to retirement vehicle with no penalties.

As soon as you take your first job, you need to be saving for retirement. If your employer does not have a retirement plan, or you happen to be self-employed, you need to put money away into a retirement account such as an IRA. There is a time value to money. The longer it has time to accrue interest, the more money you will have in the end. The difference between saving money over 30 years versus 20 years is amazing when it comes to a final total – even if the amount saved was exactly the same.

Build up your credit without ruining it. When you want to make a big purchase, you want a good credit rating that states you have borrowed before and are responsible. Having this good standing allows for a larger loan at a better interest rate.

One of the easiest ways to get credit is through a credit card. It is also very dangerous. If you take the card, make sure that you are making the monthly payments on a timely basis. Do not go wild and let your spending get out of control. Make every single purchase with your budget in mind.

CASE STUDY: DIANE PEARSON

The common misconception is that the proper payment is the minimum payment. The problem with this idea is that if you only make the minimum payment, not only will you never pay off the credit card, you will not pay enough to cover the interest for the month. Debt has to stay in control. If control is a personal problem, do not get a credit card.

Not all debt is bad. Buying a house is good debt. It is a good use of your money because you are not dipping into your savings or portfolio to make the monthly payments. Instead, you are using your day-to-day cash flow. You would either be paying rent or a mortgage out of your monthly income. As long as you can afford the monthly payments out of your regular income, a home is a good idea.

If you find yourself in debt or with a poor credit rating, there are steps take. First, you need to admit that you have a problem.

Then you need to decide if you can handle that problem alone or if you need credit counseling.

The next step is checking your credit report. There may be information reported as yours that is someone else's. Someone's credit information may end up on your report if they have a similar name.

Finally, you need to come up with a payment plan to get rid of the outstanding debt. After you have come up with that plan, you have to stick to it.

Financial mistakes are easy to make and harder to fix. That is why it is important to have a financial advisor that you trust. I recommend that if you have no knowledge on how to start a savings plan, develop a portfolio, or open an IRA, talk with someone. Your bank broker is an excellent starting point.

After you have $50,000 or more in savings vehicles, talk to someone who has more experience making investment decisions who can invest for education funds; do a survivor analysis for life insurance; and help you with disability insurance. After you own property or have a savings account, you need to have a will. This entails estate planning.

CASE STUDY: DIANE PEARSON

Most people believe that estate planning is only for the wealthy. However, every person has an estate plan. It is written by your state. In Pennsylvania if you are married and have no children, half of your money and property will go to your spouse plus an additional $30,000. The remainder will go to your parents. Every state is different, but your assets will pass to others according to state law – unless you have your own estate plan.

Estate planning also allows you to name a Power of Attorney, someone you trust to act on your behalf regarding financial issues and health care issues. You may think this is unnecessary, but if you are in surgery and the doctor discovers something, he will come out to talk with your spouse. Legally, the doctor can do what he feels is best and leave your spouse with no choices – unless your spouse is your health care Power of Attorney. Without one, your spouse simply cannot act on your behalf.

Your estate will also include your living will—"End of Life Document." It allows you to make decisions concerning your health if you are mentally incapacitated. You could stipulate that you want pain meds but no dialysis, or that you do not want to be put on a respirator.

Financial planners can also help you determine your insurance needs. Most people need disability insurance and an umbrella policy from a liability standpoint. Spouses need life insurance as well.

When you are over 50, you may need long-term care insurance. If you are between 50 and 70, it makes sense. When you are past 70 the premiums will be large and may not be cost effective. At retirement age, most people can drop long-term care insurance and rely on Medicaid.

After reaching $50,000 in savings vehicles, you need to think about your investments. Financial advisors can help you determine what is best for your needs and goals. Without an advisor, you may find yourself making one of these investing mistakes:

- Hearing a tip at a cocktail party and acting on it without doing any research.

CASE STUDY: DIANE PEARSON

- Putting all your eggs in one basket.

- Listening to a financial advisor on TV and following his advice, which cannot be personalized for you.

Your financial investments should be planned to fit your goals. Be aware that no investment is totally safe or guaranteed. Many advisors have told their clients that corporate bonds are safe. They are not. Ask anyone who worked at Enron.

There are investment vehicles that are safer than others. Treasury Bonds are safest because the monetary system of the United States would have to go under for them not to have value. CDs and savings accounts are also safer than others as long as the interest rate you are earning is keeping up with inflation.

Riskier investments include those with many advanced investing techniques. Options, futures, and derivatives are risky because they are intense and ever changing. Another risky investment is a 412(i). The investment is a life insurance plan put into a retirement plan. They are very volatile.

The industry has changed the last couple of years with banks going into financial planning. In fact, many people hang their hat on the title of financial advisor. Unless all of the following items are being accounted for, these "planners" may not understand your situation and give you unsound advice.

Cash Flow Analysis:

- Financial statements—balance sheet (net worth) tax projection, education projection.

- Retirement projection.

- Survivor analysis—insurance.

- Evaluate all current estate documents—are they up-to-date or should anything be changed? Or get one created with a lawyer, so that it all fits into the plan.

CASE STUDY: DIANE PEARSON

- Existing investments.

- This is why using a certified financial planner is a good idea.

Legend Financial Advisor, Inc.®
Diane M. Pearson, CFP™, CDFA™
Wealth Advisor and Shareholder
5700 Corporate Drive, Suite 350
Pittsburgh, PA 15237
412-635-9210 (phone) • 412-635-9213 (fax)
dpearson@legend-financial.com
www.legend-financial.com

A Typical Budget

To see the budget process in action, here is an example of a couple with three young children.

1. Determine Income:

The husband makes $38,000 a year after taxes.
The wife works part-time and makes $10,000 a year after taxes.

They do not have any investments or other sources of income.
Their monthly income is $48,000 divided by 12, which is $4000.

2. Expenses
Both fixed and variable:

Savings	$500
Groceries	$500
Rental insurance	$100
Rent	$750

Electricity.	$150
Gas	$50
Basic telephone service	$30
Internet access	$25
Household repairs	$50
Dry cleaning	$20
Credit card expenses	$100
Student loans	$65
Car insurance	$100
Car payments	$200
Car maintenance	$50
Gasoline	$80
Parking	$30
Medication	$50
Medical Insurance	$385
Dental insurance	$50
Miscellaneous Household Items (shampoo, soap, toilet paper, and light bulbs)	$100

Total Fixed & Variable Expenses $3,385
     Discretionary spending is: $4000 - $3385 = $615
(See the Budget Appendices for a Simple Budget Form.)

Budgeting and Other Considerations When Starting a Business

Personal income will be affected when starting a new business, particularly if any personal finances are invested. Additionally, there may be no source of income during the initial three to six months. Consider where the money will come from while the business is getting off the ground and how benefits — health, auto, and life insurance will be paid.

Due to these factors, adequate planning, budgeting, and saving should be done prior to starting the business to have a pool of funds to support personal expenses.

The first step is tracking monthly expenses on a daily basis to determine actual personal costs. Be sure to include buffers for emergency or surprise expenses.

Once there is a clear idea where monthly expenses go, create a budget for the period that income may be affected. Pay off any outstanding debt, home, or car loans to diminish payments during this critical period.

Many new business owners overlook the importance of having sustainable funds during this critical period. The result is looking for outside employment while still maintaining the business.

First-time business owners may need to obtain a business loan. The bank or credit union will evaluate the application based on personal credit rating because of the company's lack of credit history.

It is best to run a credit report check in the event of errors and flaws. There have been cases where loans were rejected because of credit report errors made by the system. (See Chapters Eight and Ten.)

If a personal guarantee is required on business loans, life insurance coverage will need to be increased to cover the amount. The increased coverage allows the family to pay off the debts in case of tragedy.

Secure a personal health insurance policy. Consider a Health Savings Account (HSA) plan with a high deductible policy coupled with a pre-tax savings plan. If the new business has employees, secure a group health insurance policy. The premiums for a small employee group will be more expensive than the per person cost of a large corporate health plan.

Secure personal disability coverage to provide income for family in the event of disability. Purchase a policy that provides funds for business overhead expenses in the event of disability, allowing the business to pay rent, utilities, employee salaries, and other fixed expenses for a period of time. With this type of policy in place, the business will be able to function for the duration of the disability. (See Chapter Six.)

Work with an estate-planning attorney to update the provisions of your will and trusts. Recognize the business as an asset. Give an executor directions regarding the buy/sell agreement, the ability to exercise stock options if any exist, and direct shares of the business to specific children who are active in the family business and other assets to those who are not active. (See Chapter Five.)

How Elder Care Affects a Budget

DEFINITION: Elder care is a wide range of services provided at home, in the community, and in residential care facilities, including assisted living facilities and nursing homes.

Elder care is commonplace in the United States because the elderly are living longer, healthier lives. This trend will continue as the baby boomers reach 65 and become part of the fastest growing segment of America's population. As more people reach their 80s and 90s, the number of elderly needing assistance with daily living increases; along with the responsibilities of those who provide care for them.

The care of an elderly parent can change personal budgets in many ways. Income might now include the parent's Social Security benefits. Personal expenses may now include the parent's Medicare deductible payments. It is important to understand the financial implications of elder care. It is wise to seek financial help from an advisor who is acquainted with the costs involved. Before seeing a financial planner about these matters, make sure the loved one has:

- A financial power of attorney

- A medical power of attorney

- A living will

If not, these need to be drawn up while the loved one is still mentally able to do so. If the loved one has these documents, be sure they do not need updating due to divorce, death of the executor, remarriage, or other life changes.

There are also insurance concerns. What kind of medical insurance does the loved one have? How long will it last? Is the loved one eligible for Medicaid or Medicare? Is the loved one properly enrolled? Is long-term care insurance in place? What does it cover? Having these policies when visiting the financial advisor is beneficial. He will be able to steer everyone towards a path that works.

Millions of older adults are eligible for federal and state benefits but are not receiving them, including assistance to pay Part B and Part D premiums for Medicare benefits. These programs can help with housing, meals, transportation, health care, prescription drug costs, legal services, and utility bills. Not being properly enrolled may add unnecessary expense to a personal budget.

The loved one may qualify for Supplemental Security Income (SSI). SSI pays a fixed amount per month in addition to the loved one's monthly Social Security benefit; and if qualified for SSI, the loved one will also qualify for food stamps.

Should I Use a Software Program?

If the process of creating a budget is discomforting, try using a software program to make the job easier. It will allow you to print out graphs and tables, and provide information for taxes. Quicken, MS Money, and Quickbooks are all affordable software programs.

Many banks are now offering free PC banking and free personal finance software. Simply dial into the bank's computer (or the bank may use web-based banking), and download the checks that have cleared your account directly into the personal finance software. Then indicate an expense category for each check.

Personal finance software can perform a basic comparison of budget versus actual expenses by category or can enter more detailed information: investments, assets, liabilities; and it can print personal financial statements showing net income and worth.

Whether personal finance software or pieces of paper and a pencil; get on the road to financial freedom by starting a budget today.

Decide where to put money to be spent and saved. Chapter Two will teach you everything you need to know about banking.

NOW YOU KNOW

1. Financial planning, by way of a budget, works for those who make thousands of dollars a year or hundreds of thousands of dollars a year. It is the first step.

2. For the purposes of a budget, it is much better to figure a lower number income and a higher output and be surprised at the end of the month with more money rather than the lack of it.

3. A budget does not have to be a straitjacket. It is a game plan that uses a top-down model. Take care of the important things first, and then allocate the remainder to spending.

4. Before starting a new business, know current budget needs. Missing this step may lead to seeking employment outside the business to pay bills.

5. Budgets are not static – they have to change when life circumstances change.

CHAPTER 2:
Understanding Banking

People need bank accounts for many reasons: paying to make bill paying easier, and because some accounts give interest on balances and help money grow.

There are different types of accounts and care must be taken to choose the most suitable. There are:

- Checking Accounts

- Savings Accounts

- Money Market Accounts

Each account provides regular statements that show the flow of money in and out, interest that has been paid, and charges that have been applied. It is important to check these statements. Many accounts allow access to online and telephone banking. Next up is the FDIC.

What is the Federal Deposit Insurance Corporation?

DEFINITION: The FDIC is the federal corporation that insures bank deposits up to $100,000 per social security number.

The FDIC was created in 1933 to provide insurance protection for depositors if their bank fails. Since 1933, the FDIC has responded to thousands of bank failures, and its insurance protection has been expanded to include accounts in savings and loans associations.

The FDIC protects up to $100,000 in a savings or checking account, certificate of deposit, or money market; and, as of April 1, 2006, up to $250,000 for IRA or Keogh accounts.

Your money is safe in a bank; it is up to you to choose an account that works for you.

Checking Account

DEFINITION: A checking account is a service provided by the bank allowing for the deposit of money and withdrawal of funds from a federally protected account.

Deposits and withdrawals are made in checking accounts. Wages, pensions, tax credits, and benefits are paid into a checking account without being charged a fee. Withdrawals, in the form of monthly drafts, are made to pay bills. Debit cards are a staple of checking accounts, allowing the user to pay bills and get cash back in stores, and to get money from Automatic Teller Machines (ATMs) that are free to use for customers of the bank. Some other cash machines will charge a fee to withdraw money; the user will be informed of this fee in advance of the transaction.

Checking accounts may also offer a low rate of interest on any money in the account. This can be good and bad. It is good to make a bit of extra money by keeping monthly spending allowance in an account. However, keeping too much money in a checking account will actually lose money since that money could be put into a higher interest paying account.

Savings Accounts

DEFINITION:	A savings account is where to put money not intended to be spent right away.

Savings accounts are designed for investing money on a regular basis, or for leaving lump sums of money for some time. Savings accounts pay interest on the money that is deposited. Taxpayers may have to pay tax on the interest received. Regular statements are issued that show the flow of money into and out of the account and all transactions for a given time. It is important to check them regularly to ensure personal records agree with the bank's records.

Money Market Account

DEFINITION:	A Money Market Account (MMA) is a premium account or a high interest savings account.

A MMA can be opened at almost any bank. The money kept in a MMA will be invested; the bank or other institution does the investing and collects the return. Money is put into Certificates of Deposit (CDs), Treasury Bills (T-Bills), or other safe financial instruments. Each is a low-risk, short-term investment. The reward for allowing the financial institution to use this money is a premium interest rate, one that is up to twice as much as a typical savings account. Like other bank accounts, a MMA from the bank is insured by the FDIC for up to $100,000.

While a MMA makes a decent low-risk investment, there are certain restrictions. The money will not be as liquid as in a regular savings account, and a MMA often requires a minimum deposit and a minimum balance. While withdrawals are allowed from a MMA, there is a limit to how many withdrawals can be made in a month's time, and withdrawals that cause the balance to go below the minimum result in penalties.

When Picking an Account, Watch the Fees

Many people think their checking account is free, but it is not. They are doing something for it to be free, such as maintaining a certain balance or paying a fee for going over their monthly allotment of checks.

The Federal Truth in Savings Act requires that a free account have no minimum balance requirement and no maintenance or activity fees. A maintenance fee is a monthly service charge that is incurred if the balance slips below a certain level. An activity fee is a charge for writing more than a specified number of checks in a month.

Free checking is not for everyone. Most free checking accounts do not pay interest, and some accounts have limitations or stipulations. A free checking account at some banks might be limited to withdrawing $300 per day at an ATM. Other banks may require that a regular payment such as a paycheck or government check be direct-deposited.

Also realize that free does not mean there cannot be other fees. There are plenty of "legitimate" fees that are charged in conjunction with a free checking account. Fees for non-sufficient funds (bounced checks), stopping payment, check printing, and closing an account early are a few examples.

Some fees surprise customers. Many banks include a debit card with free checking accounts. Unfortunately, more people are finding that their bank charges a fee every time they swipe their cards at a cash register. When applying for any checking account, ask for a copy of the bank's fee schedule if one is not supplied.

Online Banking

DEFINITION:	Online banking is the practice of making bank transactions or paying bills via the Internet. (Yes, that means there is no need to leave the house or even buy stamps.)

Online and telephone banking allow access to statements at any time.

Identity fraud and card theft are becoming more common with an increase in fraudulent transactions. The easiest way to detect these transactions is to check statements regularly.

After registering for an online account, you will be issued a unique password for access. Bill payment, money transfer between accounts, and application for credit cards or loans can be done online. More importantly, you can check bank statements regularly.

Telephone Banking

DEFINITION:	Telephone banking is just like online banking, except banking is done by phone.

Telephone banking allows access to accounts 24 hours a day, 365 days a year. Most everyday transactions can be carried out over the telephone after answering some simple security questions that allow access to the account. Benefits of both online and telephone banking include:

- Obtaining up to the minute balance on accounts

- Paying bills

- Transferring funds to other banks

- Setting up, amending, or canceling standing orders

- Canceling direct drafts

- Stopping checks from being paid

- Requesting statements

- Ordering new checks

- Notifying the bank of an address change

- Reporting stolen cards

How to Use an ATM

DEFINITION: An ATM is a computerized machine designed to dispense cash, take deposits, transfer money between accounts, and issue account balances.

ATMs are all over the globe, making cash available 24 hours a day, 7 days a week.

Originally, ATM cards could be used only at ATMs. Now, they have a debit feature, allowing for payment of purchases. As debit cards they have a Visa or MasterCard logo and can be used anywhere Visa or MasterCard is accepted. Unlike a credit card that bills for purchases once a month, purchases paid for with a debit card are deducted directly from the checking account.

ATMs provide convenience—with a price tag: fees. Fees are charged when using an ATM of a bank other than your own. Avoid these fees by planning ahead. Withdraw enough money from your paycheck to last until the next payday.

If low on cash, stop at your bank's ATM to refuel your wallet.

The Bank Statement

Each month, the bank sends a checking account statement. Along with this statement are the canceled checks or copies.

DEFINITION:	The statement is the bank's record of all activity that occurred in the checking account, including checks written, deposits, ATM withdrawals, and fees.

The bank account statement gives a detailed review of account activity for the month. For savings and money market accounts, it can be once a month or once a quarter. When the statement arrives, look near the top of it for the starting and ending dates— the period the statement covers.

Get your checkbook register and match every debit and credit on the statement with the register.

It is crucial to review the statement. Any discrepancies need to be reported to the bank. You have 60 days from the date of the statement to report discrepancies to the bank; otherwise, the bank has no obligation to conduct an investigation.

DEFINITION:	A statement summary is often found on the first page of the bank summary. It gives an overview of the account: the beginning and ending balances for the statement period, total deposits, total withdrawals, and service fees.

The largest section of the statement is the transaction description. It details account activity—deposits, withdrawals, and fees. Each statement will display the type of account—free checking or interest-bearing account.

Note all fees listed on the bank statement. They may be listed separately or included in the chronology of the account's monthly activity. Common fees are account maintenance, for simply having the account, and non-sufficient funds (NSF), to cover bounced checks. If there are unexplained fees on your statement, notify the bank branch. Banks make mistakes. Check the statement to see how the checks are listed, by the date they were written, or by date paid. Understanding how checks are listed makes it easier to reconcile the account.

Keep the Checkbook Balanced

Record every transaction in the check register, including ATM deposits and withdrawals, and be sure to keep a running account balance after each transaction.

To learn how to balance a checkbook, see the Basic Banking Appendices.

How Overdraft Protection Works

Sign up for overdraft protection.

DEFINITION:	An account balance becomes negative when more money is not available for all withdrawals. Overdraft protection will automatically transfer money from a line of credit or another account to cover the negative balance. Overdraft protection prevents overdraft charges, also known as non-sufficient fund (NSF) charges.

Open another account—savings, credit card, personal line of credit, or home equity line of credit—to have overdraft protection. As long as funds in the other account can cover the check, there is no NSF charge or bounced-check fee from the business that received the check.

What is ChexSystems?

When you apply for a checking account, the bank runs your application information through ChexSystems. The bank does this to weed out check bouncers and cheats.

DEFINITION: ChexSystems is like credit information bureaus. They keep tabs on people who "mishandle checking and savings accounts."

Any name that winds up in the ChexSystems database will have difficulty opening a bank account. A negative ChexSystems report stays in the database for five years and prevents you from opening a checking account.

Financial institutions lose billions of dollars each year due to check fraud and abuse, which is why 80 percent of these institutions belong to the ChexSystems network.

Tips for staying out of the ChexSystems database:

- Do not write checks without having money in the account to cover them.

- Ask the bank or credit union how long it takes for deposits to be credited to accounts.

- Keep track of balances and reconcile your checkbook with the bank's statement.

- Before closing a checking account, make sure all checks have cleared, all automatic debits have stopped, and all fees are paid.

NOW YOU KNOW

1. There are many different types of bank accounts available. Choose one that suits your needs.

2. When applying for free checking be sure to receive a copy of the bank's fee schedule. If one is not offered, ask for it.

3. Identity fraud and card theft are becoming more common with an increase in fraudulent transactions. The easiest way to detect these transactions is to check statements regularly.

4. The monthly bank account statement gives a detailed review of the activity in the account for a specific time. Make sure personal records match the bank's records.

5. For questions about ATM, debit cards, point-of-sale debit transactions, and other electronic banking transactions, there are 60 days from the date of the statement to report it to the bank or the bank has no obligation to conduct an investigation.

6. When the statement arrives, look near the top of it for the starting and ending dates. Get the checkbook register and match every debit and credit on the statement with the register.

7. Eighty percent of banking institutions belong to the ChexSystems network.

CHAPTER 3:
Why Save and How

When day-to-day finances are under control, focus on long-term financial goals. Without these goals and a plan for meeting them, financial freedom will remain just a dream.

Why Save

Living in the moment sounds wonderful, yet leaves the future uncertain. Take pleasure in the fact that you are meeting your financial goals and preparing for a successful future.

Four Simple Steps for Setting Financial Goals

Step 1: Identify and write down financial goals.

DEFINITION:	Financial goals are personal targets that are set throughout life. They fall into short-term, medium-term, and long-term categories.

To write down goals there must be a desire to achieve them. Napoleon Hill, in his best selling book, *Think and Grow Rich*, said it this way:

"The starting point of all achievement is desire. Keep this constantly in mind. Weak desires bring weak results, just as a small amount of fire makes a small amount of heat."

Whether saving to: send children to college; buy a new car; put a down payment on a house; go on vacation; pay off credit card debt; or plan for retirement, there must be desire to achieve that goal. Write down your goal.

Step 2: Determine Financial Goals

Break down each financial goal into several short-term (less than one year), medium-term (one to three years), and long term (five years or more) goals.

- **Short-term goals** cover buying a new set of tires or getting a new computer. They are useful because they are met within a matter of months.

- **Medium-term goals** take a little longer, and need planning to happen. They include paying for the next few years of school or buying a car.

- **Long-term goals** include retirement and estate plans. Because these goals require the most money, they also require the most time and planning.

After setting goals, define the steps along the way. What events must happen for these goals to become reality?

After defining these steps, do the following:

- Determine the cost of each step and the final cost of the goal.

- Estimate a time frame for each step and the final goal.

- Prioritize the goals.

Stephen Covey, author of *The Seven Habits of Highly Effective People* said:

"All things are created twice. There is a mental or first creation, and a physical or second creation of all things. You have to make sure that the blueprint, the first creation, is really what you want, that you have thought everything through. Then you put it into bricks and mortar. Each day you go to the construction shed and pull out the blueprint to get marching orders for the day. You begin with the end in mind."

Step 3: Educate Yourself.

Common ways to reach financial goals are cutting back on expenditures, finding a better job, working more than one job, saving, and spending. There are many ways to reach these goals: read this book and other books; talk with those "in the know;" and surf the Internet for tips and inspiration. Come to understand the different ways to reach personal goals, make educated decisions. These decisions will help increase net worth, and thus achieve goals.

Step 4: Evaluate progress.

After having a plan of action and beginning the steps, be sure to review it weekly, monthly, or quarterly, but do not go more than six months without reviewing.

Reviewing determines whether the program is working. If satisfactory progress is not being made on a particular goal, re-evaluate the approach and make changes as necessary.

Look at all the factors that are hindering accomplishment of this goal and develop a plan to overcome them.

Do not let the goal fade away. Figure out what needs to be done to accomplish it. Creating a financial plan is different for each person. The strategy one develops is based on education, age, family history, job, personal tendencies, and other factors. Some strategies are simple: save ten percent in a retirement plan until it is time to retire. Others need to be more complex.

Creating a financial plan also depends on personality type. Some people read 100 books and never get anywhere; others can read one and change the course of their financial life.

There are no hard and fast rules for implementing a financial plan. It is important to act now.

The Earning Power of Saving

Benjamin Franklin said, "A penny saved is a penny earned." In today's world he is wrong. A penny saved is more than a penny earned when considering income taxes.

Assume that the government takes 50 percent of earnings for taxes; many people are in the 28 percent tax bracket and by the time sales, property, state, and gasoline taxes are factored, the tax bracket nears 50 percent. Therefore, take home pay for $1,000 would be $500. When this check is cashed, it is time to budget. Account for savings, fixed bills, and variable bills. Next is discretionary spending. The cost of a night at the movies is about $40 — two tickets, popcorn and drinks, and the babysitter. By being frugal, opting for a movie from the video store and soda and microwave popcorn from the grocery store, spending is reduced to about $10. This arrangement saves $30.

To earn an extra $30, one would have to earn $60 so that the government could get its share. By saving money instead of spending, money doubles. In essence, Franklin's saying has changed to "a penny saved is two pennies earned," which translates to "save smarter, not work harder."

The easiest way to save money is to spend less. Going to the movies twice a month rather than weekly saves $60 a month, which saves $720 for the year. This savings negates the need to earn an extra $1,400 to pay for it and taxes.

This kind of spending and saving separates millionaires from the non-millionaires. In the 1996 book, *The Millionaire Next Door*, Thomas J. Stanley and William D. Danko studied prices paid by millionaires for typical purchases:

Highest price paid by the average millionaire for

Man's Suit	$399
Wristwatch	$235
Pair of Shoes	$140
New automobile	$29,000

The point is millionaires spend less than they can afford and thus save money.

Easy Ways to Save

Our society is a "spend and throw away" society. It is necessary to make decisions that go against this idea of spend, spend, spend. These are viable ways to save money that are not drastic. In fact, they are quite simple.

Buy in Bulk

DEFINITION: Buying in bulk is purchasing a large quantity of the same item at one time, often for a discounted price.

Buying in bulk saves in two ways. The first is obvious: cheaper prices. A large bottle of shampoo costs less than two smaller bottles. Warehouse clubs have become popular because the larger the quantity, the lower the price.

I recently checked prices at one of the clubs in my area and found that I could buy 300 tablets of my over-the-counter allergy medication for what 60 pills cost me at a pharmacy. The savings on just the allergy medication alone paid for the club's membership fee.

The other way to save is not as obvious, but just as effective. It has to do with inflation. Buying enough toothpaste or shower gel or any product to last three years will guarantee savings. Product price will naturally increase over time due to inflation.

Buying soap in bulk is not going to make you an instant millionaire, but buying a large number of products in bulk will save several hundred dollars a year. By using sales and buying in bulk, you can save 40 percent or more on the items you use every day. If you had a way to invest $1,000 for a 40 percent return, you would jump on it. So, why not save 40 percent on groceries and household goods and put that $1,000 away in an account?

Stop Using Credit Cards

Not paying interest on credit cards is like earning that money. Having $1,000 on a credit card at 20 percent interest and $1,000 in the bank earning 2 percent interest produces an 18 percent loss of earnings. That is $180 a year. Having $3,000 in credit card debt at 20 percent and no savings is a loss of $600 a year. It is essential to stop using credit cards and pay them off.

Pay credit cards off each month to save the interest. Look for a card that pays a rebate or gives points toward some other benefits. Do not use a card with a yearly fee. That fee is adding more interest or obliterating any benefits that the company offered.

Travel Cheap

Never pay full price on airline tickets or hotel rooms unless it is an emergency. There are several services available on the Internet that offer cheaper airfares and hotel rooms than the posted rate. By using **www.priceline.com**, I have stayed in a four-star, two-room hotel suite for 33 percent of the posted cost. My service was the same, and the amenities were the same, yet my trip was better because I knew that I had saved money. Other Internet services include **www.Expedia.com**, **www.Orbitz.com**, and **www.Cheaptickets.com**.

New Cars are No-No's

Buying a new car is like flushing money down the toilet. Cars are not an investment. They lose money over time. Instead, buy a used car at a reasonable price. Pay with cash. If borrowing is the only option, use home equity. It guarantees a low rate of interest and tax deductions on the interest paid.

Know the cost of insurance before buying a car. Comprehensive and collision insurance premiums are calculated by looking at the vehicle's loss history: how often that model is stolen, and how much it costs to repair or replace it after an accident.

Although many of these ratings are not publicly available, price quote shop. Ask about several car models and determine which one has the best rates. If one car saves $500 a year, owning that car for six years will save $3,000. (See Chapter Six for more details on buying car insurance.)

Pay Less for Phones

Another area where most people spend too much money is on their phone service. When was the last time you actually looked at your phone bill? For most people, the answer is, "um......well......" If you fall into this category, you need to look. How else will you know if you are paying too much? And if you do not know how much you are currently paying, how can you know if there are other options out there that suit you better and cost less?

- How much are you paying for call waiting? Do you use it? How much extra do you pay for caller ID? Do you need it? Does your answering machine have it built in?

- How much do you pay for call forwarding? When was the last time you needed the service?

- Do you pay long distance per call or as a monthly fee? Which way would be cheaper? Do you know?

Phone services have changed recently. Compare your service to others. If you are paying more than five cents a minute on long distance, you are overpaying. Consider dropping your long distance and use a phone card. Bundling services are another option: combining home phone, cell phone, and long distance with DSL Internet service. Another option is dropping your home phone.

Finally, you might want to check out Voice Over Internet Protocol (VOIP).

DEFINITION:	VOIP is a way to take phone call signals and turn them into digital signals that can be sent over the Internet.

VOIP allows anyone with high-speed Internet to add a phone service through the Internet. It only requires a high-speed connection, a VOIP router, and a regular telephone.

VOIP is inexpensive, ranging from $15 to $30 per month, and includes unlimited local and long distance calling.

Comparison Shop

DEFINITION:	Comparison Shopping is checking out many different stores in order to find the best price, or sometimes the best service.

Comparison shopping used to be difficult. There were sales fliers to collect and compare and road trips from store to store. Thanks to the Internet, a mouse click has replaced all that work. With the Internet, going online and checking out prices of dress pants for work at every department store in the area is a snap. Not only is comparison shopping easier, there are savings through the non-use of gasoline. You can even buy what you need online at a savings without leaving the house.

Buy Used

With the Internet, buying used is easier. No more hunting down bargains at thrift stores—look online at places like **www.Amazon. com, www.eBay.com, www.Craigslist.org, www.Overstock.com.**

Are there good deals out there? I recently bought my daughter a book that she needed for school. At the local bookstore, it would cost me $15.95. I bought the book used on Amazon for $5, including shipping. Not only did I save almost $11, I had it shipped right to my door and did not have to spend my time or my gas to get it. I do the same thing with Christmas, birthday, and some of my general shopping.

Be aware, used items still must be researched.

Just because an item is being sold used on the Internet does not guarantee it will be at a reduced price. In fact, it can cost more than new at a local store.

Use Coupons

The Internet is a good source for finding valuable coupons. By looking at a grocery store flyer online, using the valued customer card, and using printed coupons found online, the grocery bill can be reduced by up to 40 percent.

Recently, I found a good deal at our local grocery store. My favorite brand of ice cream was on sale for $2.50 per half gallon; a half price deal as long as I used my valued customer card. Then, I looked online and found a coupon for $2 off. The end result was I got ten half-gallons of ice cream for five dollars.

Although I often make my meals from scratch to save money, I do like to have a few items on hand for those overwhelming days. I like DiGiorno's frozen pizza, but it is more expensive than I like to pay. Using coupons and a valued customer rate, I was able to get these pizzas for $3 each. Now, I have several in the freezer and I will not have to buy another for a long time. By then, another good special should be available.

Sometimes I find coupons for ten percent off my grocery bill, or ones that offer a pound of produce free, or $2 off my next deli purchase. When using coupons, it is not unusual for me to save up to 50 percent on my grocery bill.

Warning: Do not buy items you normally do not buy. Saving 50 cents on a $2 item still costs you $1.50.

Save on the Electric Bill

Saving electricity saves money. Using insulation, weather stripping, and energy saving light bulbs can reduce the electric bill by up to 35 percent.

Other electric saving tips include:

- Change the furnace filter every 30 days.

- Install ceiling fans to keep the AC and heat from running as long.

- When using the dishwasher, do not use heat dry. Instead open the dishwasher to air dry.

- Wash clothes in cold water as much as possible.

- Place two or three dry hand towels in with a load of wet clothes. This cuts drying time in half.

- Turn heat down a few degrees at night.

- During summer, set the thermostat at 78 degrees Fahrenheit or higher so the air conditioner will run less. During winter, turn the set temperature down. Every degree the thermostat's set temperature is lowered in winter or raised in summer saves three percent of energy costs over a 24-hour period.

- Wash only full loads of laundry and dishes.

- Cook on an outdoor grill during the warm months.

- Turn off lights when not using.

- Turn down the water heater temperature to 120 degrees Fahrenheit.

- Close the curtains and lower the blinds on the sunny side of the house.

- Use the microwave oven rather than electric stove. Microwave ovens consume 90 percent less energy.

- If the home has a fireplace, be sure the damper is closed tightly when not in use.

No Need to Buy Name Brands

Back to the DiGiorno, if it was not on such a super sale, I would have gotten the store name pizza that tastes almost as good and is often half the price. Advertising costs are lower for store-brand products and these savings are passed on to the consumer.

Split the Difference

Prescriptions cost less by receiving double strength pills from the pharmacy and cutting them in half. A prescription of 40 mg of one medication is often not double the price of a prescription of twice the amount of 20 mg of the same medicine.

Many doctors understand the extraordinary cost of prescription medicines and are willing to work with the patient by giving double strength pills that can be cut. However, for medications that are addictive, the doctor will not be willing to do so.

Another savings option is prescriptions by mail for those medicines taken on a ongoing basis. Many insurance companies give a greater discount for ordering a 90-day-supply of medicine.

For instance, my current insurance gives me a $25 deductible on my name brand medication if I buy it one month at a time. If I choose to buy it through the mail in a 90-day supply, my deductible is $40. By ordering this way, I save $35, or $150 a year. If I have three different medications, my savings would be $450 a year.

Do These Things Actually Add Up?

Here is a look at a yearly savings:

- Eat out one less time per month: $360

- Pay $5 less on insurance per month: $60

- Go to the movies one less time per month: $180

- Buy toilet paper in bulk: $25

- Drop monthly long distance and use a phone card instead: $240

- Buy one ongoing prescription through the mail instead of monthly: $150

- Use coupons and valued customer cards at the grocery store: $240

The total saved is $1,255 a year. That is quite a bit of money. And these results do not include credit card interest savings, any energy savings, buying used, or any inflationary savings.

Look around. See what can be done cheaper. Every dollar saved is two dollars less needed to be earned.

Now that you see why you need to save and how to save without starving or living in a box, Chapter Four will show you how to get into the habit of saving and why starting early is so important.

NOW YOU KNOW
1. Without a financial plan, the future is left to chance.
2. To save money, set financial goals. Without these goals, the "Why save?" question simply makes no sense.
3. There are many ways to reach financial goals. The most common are cutting back on expenditures, finding a better job, working more than one job, saving, and spending less than you earn.
4. Understanding different ways to reach financial goals, helps in making educated decisions.
5. Creating a financial plan is different for each person. The strategy one develops will be built based on education, age, family history, job, and personal tendencies.
6. Our society is a spend and throw away society. Make decisions that go against this idea of spend, spend, spend.
7. By using sales and buying in bulk, there is a 40 percent or more savings on the items.
8. Be sure to pay off credit cards each month to save on interest charges.
9. Never pay full price on airline tickets or hotel rooms unless it is an emergency.
10. Cars are not an investment. They lose money over time.

11. Paying more than five cents a minute on long distance is paying too much.

12. When using coupons, buy only what you would normally buy. Saving 50 cents on a $2 item still costs $1.50.

13. Saving electricity saves money. Using insulation, weather stripping, and energy-saving light bulbs can reduce the electric bill by up to 35 percent.

14. Consider getting prescriptions by mail for a 90-day supply. Many insurance companies give a greater discount.

CHAPTER 4:
The Habit of Saving and Starting Early

Compound Interest Works When You Start Early

DEFINITION:	Compound interest is interest on interest. In other words, a dollar in a savings account with interest compounded will receive interest not just on the initial dollar deposited, but also interest on all the interest earned during the life of the deposit.

When new interest is calculated, it is based not only on the principal, but also on the interest that has been added to the principal. So, $1,000 in the bank at 5 percent interest earns $50 the first year. In the second year, it earns 5 percent interest on the original $1,000 and on last year's interest for a total of $52.50 in interest. Over a 30-year period, instead of gaining just $50 a year in interest equaling $1500 plus the original investment of $1,000 for a total of $2500, the compounded savings will equal $4,322 — nearly $2,000 more. Because of compounding, wealth does not grow in a straight line; it grows exponentially.

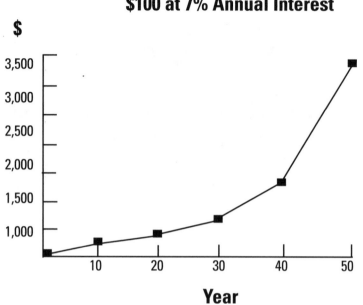

$100 at 7% Annual Interest

This means the money is growing faster and faster at the end. That is why saving $500 a month for 30 years produces more than saving $1,000 a month for 15 years. In either case, $15,000 is put into savings. However, saving $500 a month over 30 years at 10 percent yields $1,239,367.43, whereas saving $1,000 a month for 15 years only yields $452,184.50. Which would you rather have?

Start Saving Now

Adding To Your Investment Monthly

Interest earned on most investments can either be paid to the investor or be reinvested. When reinvesting the interest earned, that interest earns more interest.

So, depositing $1,000 and adding nothing to it for 30 years at a 10 percent interest rate, the money will grow to $17,449.40. The plan, of course, is to add money monthly.

Your total is $1,039,646 after 30 years.

Below is what happens to savings by adding $500 a month over 30 years at an interest rate of 10 percent:

Savings Balance by Year

YEAR	ADDITIONS	INTEREST	BALANCE
			$0
1	$6,000	$320	$6,320
2	$6,000	$952	$13,273
3	$6,000	$1,648	$20,920
4	$6,000	$2,412	$29,332
5	$6,000	$3,254	$38,586
6	$6,000	$4,179	$48,765
7	$6,000	$5,197	$59,961
8	$6,000	$6,316	$72,278
9	$6,000	$7,548	$85,826
10	$6,000	$8,903	$100,729
11	$6,000	$10,393	$117,122
12	$6,000	$12,032	$135,154
13	$6,000	$13,836	$154,990
14	$6,000	$15,819	$176,809
15	$6,000	$18,001	$200,811
16	$6,000	$20,401	$227,212

17	$6,000	$23,041	$256,253
18	$6,000	$25,946	$288,199
19	$6,000	$29,140	$323,339
20	$6,000	$32,654	$361,993
21	$6,000	$36,520	$404,513
22	$6,000	$40,772	$451,285
23	$6,000	$45,449	$502,733
24	$6,000	$50,594	$559,327
25	$6,000	$56,253	$621,580
26	$6,000	$62,478	$690,058
27	$6,000	$69,326	$765,384
28	$6,000	$76,859	$848,243
29	$6,000	$85,145	$939,387
30	$6,000	$94,259	$1,039,646

Now you can see the benefit of using compounded interest every month.

Save Money Automatically

You cannot miss something you never had. If savings are taken directly out of the paycheck without ever bringing it home, it is unlikely to be missed. Bringing it home and then trying to put it away leads to temptation.

There is a good chance that your employer has a job savings program: retirement savings, 401(k), stock options, or other similar options. Putting money into one of these programs is an excellent savings option.

Most people have their paycheck direct-deposited into their checking account. Have the check split into two accounts or have an automatic withdrawal from your savings into checking. Either way, the money will not be seen or missed.

Saving money involves forgoing immediate gratification. It demands discipline and requires sacrifice. Saving is an extremely empowering behavior. It is a key to making dreams come true. Saving makes us strong. It provides direction and focus. It is a life strategy to determine what we value and gives us the means to obtain it.

Saving For College Expenses

Parents should expect to pay at least half to two-thirds of their children's college costs through a combination of savings, current income, and loans. Gift aid from the government, the colleges and universities, and private scholarships accounts for only about a third of total college costs.

Parents should start saving for their child's education early. Time is a valuable asset. The sooner saving for college starts, the more time for money to grow.

Even a modest weekly or monthly investment can grow to a significant college fund by the time the child is ready for college. Saving $50 a month from birth would yield about $20,000 by the time the child turns 17, assuming a 7 percent return on investment. Saving $200 a month would yield almost $80,000.

It is less expensive to save for college than to borrow. Either way, a portion of income is being set aside to pay for college; when saving, the money earns interest; when borrowing, money goes to interest.

Even if college is just a year or two away, it is never too late to start saving. Under current financial aid formulas, there are significant benefits to saving money in the parent's name, despite the tax savings of the child's lower tax bracket. Money in the student's name is assessed more heavily than that in the parent's. Students are expected to contribute 20 percent of their assets, while parents only weigh in at 5.5 percent. That is why it is better to save for college in the parent's name.

Section 529 Plans

DEFINITION:	A Section 529 Plan, named for the section of the Internal Revenue Code, is a savings plan for college expenses.

Section 529 plans are among the best ways for saving for a child's college education. There are two types of section 529 plans: pre-paid tuition and college savings.

Prepaid tuition plans are guaranteed to increase in value at the same rate as college tuition. If a family purchases shares worth half a year's tuition at a state college, these shares will always be worth half a year's tuition—even ten years later, when tuition rates may have doubled. Most plans require that either the account owner or the beneficiary be a state resident when the account is opened.

Anybody can contribute to a prepaid tuition plan, including grandparents and friends. If the child dies or decides not to go to college, the plan can be transferred to another member of the family. The money in the plan is controlled by the account owner, not the child.

Section 529 college savings plans are tax-exempt with a low impact on need-based financial aid eligibility. Unlike prepaid tuition plans, there is no lock on tuition rates and no guarantee. Investments are subject to market conditions, and the savings may not be sufficient to cover all college costs. With this added risk comes the opportunity for earning greater returns.

Section 529 college savings plans are similar in many ways to

401(k) and IRAs, with much higher contribution limits and more favorable tax status.

Coverdell Education Savings Accounts (ESAs)

Coverdell Education Savings Accounts (ESAs) were previously known as Education IRAs. They are similar to Roth IRAs. Both allow the investor to make an annual non-deductible contribution to a specially designated investment trust account. The account will grow free of federal income taxes, and withdrawals from the account will be completely tax-free as well.

Qualified higher education expenses include expenses for tuition, fees, books, supplies, and equipment required for enrollment or attendance. If the child is enrolled at least half time at an eligible college, certain room and board expenses qualify as well.

Rethinking Budget and Savings after a Divorce

A divorce brings up a host of financial situations that need to be addressed. From making sure there is insurance coverage (many couples are on one healthcare plan together), to reviewing the accrued retirement savings. And there are additional issues such as tax implications and estate planning issues. An emergency reserve should be established — at least three months of income in savings. Make sure healthcare needs are met and that assets are insured properly.

After those goals have been met, start thinking about retirement goals. Switching from a dual to a single income might seem daunting, but every little bit put away for the future can affect your retirement date. Diversify investments by putting them in a range of investment options as opposed to just one or two.

NOW YOU KNOW

1. If you want the money in your savings account to work in your favor, start saving immediately. The younger you start, the more money you will have in the end. One reason to start early is to start good habits.

2. Due to compounding, wealth does not grow in a straight line; it grows exponentially.

3. Having savings taken directly out of the paycheck without ever bringing it home decreases the likelihood of the savings being missed.

4. Just as with budgets, savings goals can change with life-changing circumstances such as divorce.

CHAPTER 5:

Do You Need a Financial Advisor?

Income and estate tax laws are always changing, and so are financial products, investment options, and risk management issues. Time and professional training are needed to keep informed. You can become ill and not able to manage your financial affairs. For all these reasons you may need a financial advisor.

What Is a Financial Advisor?

DEFINITION:	A financial advisor is a trained professional who can help with personal finances and plan for future finances.

Financial advisors practice comprehensive planning, look at the whole picture, and think about now and the future. Comprehensive planning does include helping to select investments, but it also includes budgeting, tax efficient investing, portfolio maintenance, and retirement planning.

The litmus test of whether advisors are right or not is to ask them if they get personally involved developing plans for their clients. Of course most of them will say yes.

If they do say yes, ask them to provide the names of five clients they currently have. If they cannot give these references, find another advisor.

Choosing a financial advisor is one of the most important steps to take when getting your financial house in order. A financial advisor will help set goals, including retirement age and the funds required to get there. The advisor will help filter through the endless stream of financial products available (the stream grows daily) and evaluate which ones will be best.

A man named Bob went to a financial advisor and received a complete review. He had all his financial statements together; he knew what he wanted in education benefits and survivor benefits. The advisor created recommendations based on his needs and wants that would enhance his situation. One week later, he called his financial advisor. "You are not going to believe this. When I got to work this morning, I had my pink slip on my desk. I was fired. However, thanks to you, I am not afraid. I know exactly what my options are." Because he knew where he was financially, he could make good decisions. Although he had enough to retire, he did not want to. Therefore, he started up his own photography studio based on his hobby instead of pursuing another high-pressure job.

Having a plan led to his peace of mind. It also led him to a new business venture based on something he had always wanted to do. Without a financial plan, this would not have been possible. The moral of the story here is to have a plan.

A financial advisor should make his clients feel comfortable and meet both their immediate and future needs.

How does a person find such an advisor? Start with friends. Ask them who they use and if the advisor is meeting their financial goals. Look in books, check out financial seminars, and read the financial newspaper columnists to find names of advisors. Gather a substantial list so that all options are apparent.

Then consider the education and reputation of each advisor, including.

- Credentials

- Number of years in business

- Experience, especially with people in similar circumstances to yours

- Schooling

- Recent employment history

- Licenses

Cross off all agents from the list who do not meet your expectations. When you find an advisor, you need to look at his or her philosophy. Does it match yours?

Develop specific questions related to your financial goals and realize your own personal style. Are you looking for a partner in managing your investments, or are you willing to give control to the advisor? Do you have any social or political beliefs that need to be considered in establishing your goals?

Look for a teacher and not a salesman. You want someone who is willing to explain the financial buzzwords, not just dazzle you with them.

Most advisors will have an introductory meeting with you at no cost. While at this meeting, decide how comfortable you feel with the advisor on both a personal and a professional manner.

To learn more about picking a financial planner, see the Advisor Appendices.

How Financial Advisors Are Paid

There are four ways that financial advisors are paid.

- **Commissions:** The advisor sells specific products and is rewarded by doing so. He is also paid for policy renewals, portfolio updates, and transactions.

- **Fee Based on Percentage of Assets:** These advisors determine their fee based on the assets in a portfolio, a very common payment arrangement. If they take 1 percent of a $100,000 portfolio, they will be paid $1,000 per year.

- **Fee Based on an Hourly Rate:** The advisor is paid by the hour of advice given.

- **Flat Fee for a Financial Plan:** This type of advisor is just a planner — someone who is willing to look over the situation and come up with a plan for a specific price.

An advisor may charge fees according to more than one of these payment methods. An advisor may be a planner who has a flat fee for a plan and then charges an hourly rate on an "as needed" basis, or charges hourly while maintaining some commission products, or charges for a plan and then charges a percentage of the portfolio yearly.

There is no right or wrong way to pay an advisor. The point is to understand what you are paying for and to be satisfied with the work he is performing for you.

Additional Financial Professionals You May Need

CPA

DEFINITION:	While a Certified Public Accountant (CPA) is always an accountant, not all accountants are CPAs. To become a CPA, an accountant must take and pass a series of rigorous tests administered by the American Institute of Certified Public Accountants.

Certified Public Accountants handle a variety of tasks. They offer basic business record keeping, auditing, and consulting work; taxes are the main reason people seek their advice. Taxes are the biggest expense a person will experience in life. Taxes are also the biggest expense after death. A CPA will help reduce this expense.

Attorney for Wills and Estate Planning

The purpose of this section is not to explain everything about wills and estate planning. To do so would take an entire book. This section is simply to show that it is necessary to have someone who knows how to help.

DEFINITION:	A will is a legal document that allows people to choose who receives their belongings and assets after death.

The simplest way to ensure that funds, property, and other items will be distributed according to personal wishes after death is to prepare a will. You need to plan your estate so that the transfer of your assets to your beneficiaries will be quick and as tax-free as possible.

DEFINITION:	Estate planning sets your affairs in order so loved ones will not be burdened with too many details after your death.

The process of estate planning includes making a list of your money and assets, such as real estate and anything else of monetary or sentimental value. It also includes making a will or establishing a trust. Wills and estate planning require an attorney; interview candidates to determine their areas of expertise. Select one who understands your interests.

Insurance Professional

Insurance agents determine the insurance you need now and in the future. Select an agent from a well-established, financially sound company with high ratings. The agent should anticipate your needs through retirement. Discuss long-term care, disability, car and medical insurance. Identify insurance beneficiaries during times of life change: marriage, divorce, children, and retirement.

Financial Counseling During a Divorce

Divorce is an emotional time. In the world of finances, it is a crucial time. Here are some steps to make the best of the situation:

1. **Share all financial information:** list all investments— stocks, bonds, mutual funds—and determine who is listed as the owner. List all debts—mortgage, car payment, and credit cards—and determine who is listed as the owner. Keep in mind, you are not trying to split up assets or debts; these lists are the basis for later actions.

2. **Establish new investment strategy**—You and your spouse may have had different investment styles. As a couple, you may have reached some common ground in

terms of your overall investment strategy, but now that you are single, you need to base investment decisions on your own risk tolerance, long-term goals, and time horizon.

3. **Evaluate insurance**—Once divorced, you may lose some protections you had while married. Consider expanding life and disability insurance.

4. **Update estate planning documents**—revise your will, living trust, and other legal documents related to your estate.

Change your beneficiaries. Review the beneficiary designations on all of your financial papers, including insurance policies, retirement plans, and annuities. Many people forget to change their beneficiaries when they divorce. Get a financial advisor and insurance agent. Chapter Six will help you get through the insurance maze so that you can ask your agent all the right questions.

NOW YOU KNOW
1. There is constant change in income and estate tax laws, financial products, investment options, and risk management issues.
2. When looking for a financial advisor look for a teacher, not a salesman—someone willing to explain the financial buzzwords, not just dazzle you with them.
3. Financial advisors will have an introductory meeting at no cost. While at this meeting, decide how comfortable you feel with the advisor on both a personal and professional manner.

4. There is no right or wrong way to pay a financial advisor. The point is to understand what you are paying for and to be satisfied with the work he or she is performing.

5. Taxes are the biggest expense a person experiences in life. Consider having a CPA.

6. Life events, such as a divorce, can result in new financial needs and questions. Seeking advice during these events is wise.

7. To be financially successful, you need help along the way. Be sure this help is from experienced, educated professionals keen to your specific financial issues.

CHAPTER 6:
Insurance You May Need

Insurance protects you financially in case of an accident or loss of property. Everybody is susceptible to these risks. Without this protection, enormous strain and long-term hardship are almost inevitable.

Luke V. Erickson, of the University of Idaho, Madison County, an expert in consumer issues, suggests that everyone needs sound health, auto, and homeowner's coverage, and that life, disability, and long-term health insurance are the biggest fluctuating needs.

Young single adults do not require much life and disability insurance as there are no dependents in the picture. Marriage changes that. There is a spouse and children to protect so that life insurance becomes a concern. Term-life insurance is the most cost effective insurance during the early years of marriage. Additionally, get disability insurance to cover bills during any periods of lost work.

By the time you are middle aged, you will still need a

considerable amount of life insurance and disability insurance, especially until the children are out on their own. If you have not built up any sort of substantial savings, it would also be a good idea to make sure the spouse is covered. Some life insurance options can be used as part of an investment portfolio, but rarely is life insurance the best option as an investment. At this point in life you will also want to consider long-term care insurance. If you are disabled in a way that leads to a long-term care facility, your savings and investments can be wiped out quickly.

When you are older (past 65), life insurance is often too costly to be of any real benefit. The same is true for long-term care. When you are able to receive Medicaid, long-term care insurance can be stopped.

A look at the various insurances:

Medical Insurance

DEFINITION:	Medical (also known as health) insurance is a contract between you and an insurance company that says that if you pay your premiums monthly, the company will pay for agreed on medical expenses.

Having no health insurance coverage means paying out-of-pocket for health care at the time of service. Paying for medical care this way can cost many thousands of dollars. Health insurance protects you financially.

By enrolling in a health care plan, you pay a monthly or quarterly fee as insurance for the time you need medical attention. When a service is provided, the health insurance organization pays some or all the fee.

For instance, some plans specify that you can visit your doctor for whatever reason by paying $20 upfront and the insurance will pay the rest. Others have an 80/20 plan in which you pay 20 percent of the bill, and insurance pays 80 percent. You must watch and be aware of what kinds of medical expenses your insurance will not pay for. For instance, some policies will not pay for mental health care or for pre-existing conditions.

Many employers offer medical insurance. Take it, even if you have to pay part of the cost. You are never going to get it cheaper than having your employer subsidize it.

Auto Insurance

DEFINITION: Auto insurance is a contract with an insurance company that can protect you against severe financial loss if you are ever in an auto accident.

All drivers must have auto insurance.

Call an auto insurance agent and be ready with a list of cars you are thinking about buying. Auto insurance agents can tell you the cost of insurance for all models before you buy.

Characteristics of the vehicle being purchased play a large role in insurance costs. Below is a list of features or types of vehicles to avoid:

- Vehicles with high horsepower

- Sports cars

- High-performance vehicles

- Luxury vehicles

- Vehicles with added technology features

- Large SUVs

- Very small vehicles

- Vehicles with a high theft history

Here are the top ways to reduce car insurance:

- **Theft Devices:** Having a theft device lowers rates.

- **Multiple Car Discount:** Sometimes insuring two cars can be the same price as insuring one. Check with your insurance agent for any discount.

- **Yearly Policies:** Choosing a yearly policy, instead of a six-month policy, can extend your savings.

- **Comprehensive Storage Coverage:** When storing your car, keep only comprehensive coverage.

- **Mileage:** By checking your mileage to and from work, you may be eligible for a discount.

- **Organization Affiliation:** Many companies offer a discount for being affiliated with certain organizations like credit unions or college sororities, or having a certain credit card.

- **Liability/Comprehensive/Collision/Medical Payments Coverages:** Comprehensive and collision insurance can be lowered by increasing your deductible. Most vehicles that are on bank loans can have up to a $1,000 deductible. Lowering your liability and medical payments could help, but only if you are having a hard time paying for your premium and is not recommended for general savings.

- **EFT Payments:** Companies are charging up to $5 for mail payments, and nothing for payments automatically deducted.

- **Defensive Driving Course:** Some companies give considerable discounts for attending defensive driving courses. Check with your state insurance commissioner, insurance company, or go online to see whether there is a benefit, whether you qualify, and where to take courses.

- **Auto/Home/Renter's Companion Policies:** You can get a 5 percent to 20 percent discount if you carry your auto and home or renter's policy with the same company.

- **Credit Rating:** Keep your credit clean. Insurance companies are checking credit and basing policy premiums on credit ratings.

- **Teenage Drivers:** Driver Education and good grades can earn a discount.

- **Rental Car:** If you have comprehensive and collision coverage on your current vehicle, you might not need rental coverage. If you have an older car, get rental coverage.

- **High Risk:** Contact your state insurance commissioner. All states have insurance for high-risk individuals who may not be able to obtain insurance elsewhere. The coverage may not be the greatest, but at least it will get you rolling again.

Life Insurance

DEFINITION: Life insurance pays money to the person named on your policy when you die as long as the premiums are kept up to date.

Life insurance provides financial security to dependents when you die. There are three types of life insurance.

- **Term** — covers a fixed period of time from one to thirty years and provides life coverage only. Upon your death, it pays the face amount of the policy to your named beneficiary. Premiums for term insurance are lowest for people in good health and under 50. After that age, premiums become progressively more expensive.

- **Whole life** — combines a term policy with an investment component. Some of the money paid into a whole life policy accumulates as guaranteed cash values. You may borrow against these cash values as a policy loan at the current policy loan interest rate or as the policy expires, take the cash. The growth in cash values is tax deferred under current federal income tax law. The amount of guaranteed cash value depends on the kind of whole life policy you have, its size, and how long you have had it.

- **Universal insurance** — is a type of whole life insurance that mixes term insurance and a savings fund, earning interest at a money market rate. You pay a yearly fee for this coverage, which includes a cost of managing the policy. Funds not paying for insurance earn tax-deferred interest.

  With a universal life policy, the premium can vary. You decide how much to pay toward insurance and toward savings. You can change the face amount of the policy, or change the amount of premium payments and how often you pay them. You must be sure your savings are enough to cover the monthly premiums for insurance and policy expenses. If they are not, the monthly charges will use up the cash value and your policy will be worthless.

  Universal life insurance has two options. **Option A**: the death benefits stay the same from year to year if you do not ask for any changes. **Option B**: the death benefits at any time is equal to the original face amount plus the policy's cash value.

(To determine how much life insurance you need, see the Insurance Appendices.)

Disability Insurance

DEFINITION: Disability insurance helps replace your income if you are unable to work due to illness or injury.

Disability insurance should be considered a necessity. Savings of six percent of annual income for ten years can be wiped out by a six-month disability.

Ask yourself this question, "Can I live without income for three months, six months, or a year?"

If the answer is no, you need disability insurance. Employers often offer this coverage via a payroll deduction, which may be tax-deductible. Disability insurance is protection for your future income. It covers your inability to earn a living wage as a result of poor health or injury.

Consider these facts:

The Social Security Administration's Disability Benefits publication claims that a 20-year-old worker has a 30 percent chance of becoming disabled before retirement age.

Government statistics from 1997 show that the same 20-year-old has only a 17 percent chance of dying before age 65 and these odds continue to decline as we live longer.

Disability insurance is more expensive than life insurance because insurance companies make a living aligning premium costs with the odds of a claim. Disability payouts are more common than life insurance payouts. Since the payouts are higher, the premiums are higher.

Short Term Disability

DEFINITION: Short-term disability insurance covers a percentage of your lost salary should injury or illness keep you from work for more than a few days.

With short-term disability, payments start when all available sick leave is exhausted. You will see a large portion of your salary early on, but payments are reduced to 60 percent of salary after a few weeks. Duration of benefits varies by policy, but six months is typical.

When it comes to missing work for six months or less, most people have a number of sources for help:

Paid Leave: Sick Leave and Emergency Leave.

- **Workers' compensation:** Employers are required to provide workers' compensation benefits. They replace a portion of your income when unable to work temporarily because of an accident that occurs in the workplace or on company time doing company work. These benefits vary dramatically by state.

- **Automobile insurance:** Auto insurance may include payments to cover medical costs and lost income.

- **Emergency savings:** Align the size of your emergency fund with the projected shortfall in your short-term disability insurance over a six-month absence. A six-month absence is likely to force you into living on only 60 percent of your current salary.

- **IRA** rules allow for disability withdrawals before age 59. You can withdraw one half without a 10 percent penalty, but you have to prove that "your condition can be expected to result in death or to be of long, continued, and indefinite duration." Withdrawals to cover short-term work absences are likely to be penalized.

  IRAs have provisions for early withdrawals without penalty, to cover substantial medical costs and health insurance premiums should you lose your job. But, these will not apply to basic living expenses over the short-term.

Long-term Disability

DEFINITION: Long-term disability insurance is a more typical insurance that protects from catastrophic illness or injury that permanently ends your ability to work.

Long-term disability policies pick up where short-term disability policies leave off.

Here are considerations when purchasing long-term disability insurance:

1. You will need 60 to 80 percent income replacement.

2. Have a policy that stays in place until you turn 65.

3. How disability is defined is crucial. It should include mental illness, stress disorders, back pain, migraines, carpal tunnel syndrome, chronic fatigue disorder, pre-existing conditions, and other medical problems.

4. Policies are classified "any occupation" or "own occupation."

Any occupation means you are disabled and unable to work in any position in your field. Own occupation means you are disabled and unable to work in your own occupation in your field.

If you are a research chemist and become unable to work, you may be able to work as an assistant making far less money. With any occupation coverage, you would have to take the lower paying job instead of getting disability.

Own occupation coverage is a better choice for high paying jobs with a broad category of workers.

Homeowner's Insurance

DEFINITION: Homeowner's insurance combines coverage against loss of property and liability insurance for accidents that happen at the home.

There are a number of fairly standard homeowner's policies. All forms of homeowner's insurance cover liability.

Forms of Coverage

The Basic Coverage Form: provides a minimal amount of coverage. It applies to your dwelling and property, and insures against fire, lightning, vandalism, malicious mischief, and extended coverage perils.

Extended coverage perils include:

- Riot

- Explosion

- Vehicles (damage inflicted by, not to a vehicle)

- Civil commotion

- Smoke

- Hail

- Aircraft

- Windstorm

- Breakage of glass that is part of the building

The Broad Coverage Form: applies to both home and property and includes all the coverage of the basic form, plus these perils:

- Falling objects

- Weight of snow, sleet, and ice

- Damage to water heating systems

- Volcanic eruption

- Damage from plumbing or appliances

- Freezing of plumbing or appliances

- Damage from artificially generated currents

Special Coverage Form: provides the most extensive coverage of all the forms. The policy covers "risks of direct loss." Any cause of loss is covered except those specifically excluded in the policy—exclusions are flood, war, or nuclear accident. Personal property is covered to the same extent as in the Broad Form.

Liability Coverage

Liability covers bodily injury to other people or damage to their property due to your neglect, while on your property. Liability may also cover the medical expenses of the injured.

How Much Homeowner's Insurance Do You Need?

If your home is financed, your lender may require that you carry enough insurance to cover the value of the dwelling and outbuildings. Insurance should cover the dwelling and personal property's worth.

Most policies are sold with a fixed amount of liability coverage. You can purchase more than the standard amount.

You want to purchase enough insurance to cover the value of all your financial assets that are vulnerable to a lawsuit. Your insurance company is liable only up to the limits of your policy. You are liable for anything above that.

Additional liability coverage is not expensive; for $10 to $12 more, you can double the standard limit.

How to Reduce Your Premiums

Here are eight ways to minimize the cost of homeowner's insurance.

1. Raise Your Homeowner's Insurance Deductible

> **DEFINITION:** Your homeowner's deductible is the amount of risk you agree to accept before the insurance company starts paying on a claim.

With the cost of homeowner's insurance escalating, it no longer makes sense to let the insurance company assume all the risk. If you have a low deductible of $50 to $100, consider raising it to at least $500 to $1,000, for a savings up to 25 percent on premiums. The trends in homeowner's insurance are for insurance companies to penalize customers who file one or more small claims. Often the premiums are raised or the policy is canceled. When looking elsewhere for coverage, homeowner may find tripled insurance rates.

2. Combine Your Homeowner's Insurance and Auto Insurance Policies

Consider buying your homeowner's and auto insurance policies from the same company. Some companies offer discounts of 5 percent to 15 percent if you buy both types of coverage from them.

Check around and make sure the price is lower than buying two policies from two different companies before making this move.

3. Ask About Other Homeowner's Insurance Discounts

Make sure you are receiving all the discounts you are due. Discounts exist for smoke detectors, deadbolt locks, security or fire alarm systems, and fire extinguishers. If you are over 55 and retired, you may qualify for an additional 10 percent discount.

4. Do Not Buy Homeowner's Insurance Coverage You Do Not Need

It makes no sense to buy insurance to protect yourself against risks you are unlikely to encounter: earthquake coverage in a non-earthquake zone, or a jewelry floater to your policy if you do not own expensive jewelry.

5. Make Your Home a Better Insurance Risk

Ask your insurance agent what you can do to reduce your premiums. Changes that reduce the risk of damage in windstorms and other natural disasters are one example. Another is updating old wiring or heating systems, reducing risk of fires.

6. Avoid Risks that Insurers Shun

Insurers are shying away from some risks; owning certain types of dogs, Rottweilers, Doberman Pinschers, or Pit Bulls can limit or void your policy; owning a swimming pool or a trampoline can increase your cost of coverage. Read all the fine print in your policy under the "Conditions and Coverages" sections so you know what is excluded from coverage. You may opt to buy additional coverage to protect yourself from certain exposures.

7. Improve Your Credit Score

Insurance companies are increasingly using credit information to price insurance policies. Do not have too many open credit accounts. Do not charge to the limits on your credit cards, and pay all your bills on time to keep your credit score healthy.

8. Shop Around for Homeowner's Insurance

Shop around for homeowner's insurance rates but realize you may be receiving a longevity discount from your current insurer. Typical discounts are 5 percent if you have been with the company for three to five years, and 10 percent for six years or more. Get quotes from three agents, and take any longevity discounts with your current insurer into consideration when you compare prices. Your state insurance department may have rate comparison information available for your state.

Renter's Insurance

DEFINITION: Renters insurance is a low-cost insurance policy which covers almost all personal property inside an apartment or rental home and liability for medical or legal expenses if a visitor is injured.

Landlords are responsible only for the building. Only you are responsible for your property.

The amount of personal property coverage you need depends on how much your property is worth. To understand your needs, ask yourself:

- How much are my belongings worth?

- Could I afford to buy it all back again if it were destroyed in a fire or stolen?

- What would I do in the event of a liability lawsuit against me?

The average person has over $20,000 worth of belongings that are not covered by a landlord's policy.

Find out how much coverage you need by taking an inventory of your possessions:

1. List each item, purchase price, and current value.

2. Total the amounts of these items for a rough idea of worth.

3. Put your inventory in a safe place away from home—a bank safe deposit box.

4. Consider taking photos of your inventory. They can help with a claim.

Coverage for certain types of property have a dollar limit in a renter's policy:

- Money, bank notes, coins

- Business property (on and off premises)

- Securities, negotiable instruments

- Watercraft, including trailers, furnishings and equipment

- Trailers (other than boat trailers)

- Jewelry and furs

- Firearms (limitation applies to theft only)

- Silverware and gold ware (limitation applies to theft only)

These properties may need special coverage.

Prepaid Legal Insurance

DEFINITION: Prepaid legal insurance uses your premiums to pay for any legal needs.

According to the American Bar Association, half of all U.S. citizens require the services of an attorney each year. Many people are now considering prepaid legal insurance. Individuals and families pay about $16 to $26 per month in exchange for legal help with traffic tickets to will writing.

Identity Theft Insurance

Identity thieves now have a faster way of assuming others' names: the Internet.

DEFINITION: Identity theft occurs when a thief assumes someone else's identity to commit fraud in that person's name without their knowledge. By the time the victim catches on, the thief is often long gone, leaving behind a trail of ruined credit, debts, and collectors.

Identity theft insurance reimburses the expenses of repairing credit reports, recovering lost wages, phone bills, mailing costs, and attorney fees depending on the policy chosen.

Do Not Buy Insurance You Do Not Need

One important way to reduce your insurance costs is to avoid purchasing policies that you do not need.

Insurance to Avoid:

1. **Comprehensive and collision** coverage for automobiles that have little or no value.

2. **Personal injury protection** coverage (PIP) or buy the minimum if you have a good health insurance policy.

3. **Roadside assistance** if you already belong to an organization that offers it.

4. **Mechanical breakdown insurance** if you own a new car or have a leased vehicle still under warranty.

5. **Rental car insurance** if you have a current full coverage policy or a credit card that already provides this insurance. Check with your agent to see how much your current policy will cover.

6. **Life Insurance** if you are single and have no dependents.

7. **Travel insurance** if your current health insurance policy covers you abroad.

8. **Extended Warranties on Appliances**. They may cost more than just buying a new one.

9. **Insurance on outstanding credit card balances**. This type of insurance can be costly and has many loopholes.

10. **Credit Insurance**, which is voluntary insurance on your mortgage. A typical life insurance policy would be a better option.

By avoiding the above policies, you will not reduce your risk and you still may experience a loss in any or all the above categories, but the risk for most is so small it is just not worth the price of the insurance.

Where to Buy Your Insurance

If you are shopping for insurance you have three choices: online, exclusive, or non-exclusive agent.

Online Insurance

Advantages would include buying insurance on your time and eliminating pushy insurance salesmen. Also, you have customer service for questions, which is what most people use after signing up with an agent anyway.

The disadvantages are that there is no discount for buying online versus using an agent and you lose that "personal touch" of service.

Local Exclusive Agent

A local exclusive agent sells insurance for one company. Advantages of an exclusive agent are that the agent has extensive training from the company, and you can get online service.

The disadvantage is that they sell for only one company, so that there is only one price tier.

Local Non-exclusive Agent

A non-exclusive agent deals with a variety of companies to tailor the best insurance policy for you. This is advantageous if you have special circumstances that make it hard for you to acquire insurance elsewhere.

The disadvantage can be higher price and a company you are not familiar with. If you choose a non-exclusive agent, it is best to check the company's ratings.

A Higher Deductible

When buying insurance, you are not insuring 100 percent of everything. The insurance policy pays your loss that exceeds a certain base amount: the deductible. The deductible is the part of the loss for which you are responsible.

Having a large cash reserve frees you to have a higher deductible on your insurance. Instead of having $100 deductible on the car maybe you can afford a $500 or $1,000 deductible. If there is an emergency, you can cover it.

Do not have a deductible so high you cannot afford it or a deductible so low that your premiums are too high; having a deductible a bit higher than the minimum may reduce insurance cost by 20 to 30 percent.

Chapter Seven will discuss retirement savings.

NOW YOU KNOW

1. Insurance protects you and your family financially against risks that put an enormous strain on you with a potential long-term hardship.

2. Medical insurance is important. Without health insurance coverage, you have to pay for health care out of your own finances at the time of service.

3. Car insurance agents can tell you the cost of insurance for the different car models before you buy.

4. There are many different ways to lower your car insurance.

5. Life insurance is necessary if you have dependents who will suffer financially if you die.

6. Just like life insurance, disability insurance is protection for your future income.

7. There are a number of standard homeowner's policies called forms. All forms of homeowner's insurance cover liability.

8. The average person has more than $20,000 worth of belongings that are not covered by a landlord's policy. This is why renter's insurance is essential.

9. According to the American Bar Association, half of America requires the services of an attorney each year.

10. Identity theft insurance reimburses the expenses of repairing credit reports, recovering lost wages, phone bills, mailing costs, and attorney fees depending on the policy chosen.

11. There are three ways to shop for insurance: Online, exclusive, or non-exclusive agent.

12. When you buy insurance, you are not insuring 100 percent of everything. You are obligated to pay a deductible.

CHAPTER 7:
Saving For Retirement

Congress allows everyone to save for retirement in a variety of ways, including Individual Retirement Accounts (IRAs), Roth IRAs, Keogh accounts for the self-employed, employer-sponsored 401(k) plans, 403 (b) annuities for nonprofit organizations, and tax-deferred annuities. These investments can be pre-tax contributions.

The financial experts consulted for this book say the time to start retirement savings is now. It does not matter whether you are single, married, divorced, middle aged, or even nearing retirement. Retirement planning is a necessity and the younger you start the process, the more time you will have to see the interest compound.

There are different ways to save for retirement.

Company Retirement Plans

Companies now offer their employees a 401(k) retirement plan after six to twelve months of service.

DEFINITION:	A 401(k) plan allows employees to save for their own retirement. This type of plan was named for section 401(k) of the Internal Revenue Code that permits employees of qualifying companies to set aside tax-deferred funds with each paycheck.

Any money put into a 401(k) is tax-free and reduces the amount of income to report to the IRS. Many employers will match contributions up to a certain amount.

Only 61 percent of those eligible to participate in a 401(k) do so. Of those people, many do not contribute the maximum allowed each year.

Contribution limit for a 401(k) is the lower of the maximum amount your employer permits as a percentage of salary (e.g., if your employer lets you contribute 4 percent of your salary and you earn pre-tax $20,000, your maximum contribution limit is $800), or the government guidelines. In 2007, the maximum allowable contribution into a 401)k) is $15,500. Each year this amount is adjusted for inflation.

With a $40,000 annual income, investing 10 percent will reduce taxable income to $36,000. If the effective income tax rate is 31 percent, the year-end tax savings will be $1,550. (Original annual income is $40,000, multiplied by the effective tax rate of 31 percent yields $12,710 for tax. The reduced taxable income, $36,000 multiplied by 31 percent yields $11,160. Subtracting $11,160 from $12,710 yields the $1550 tax savings.)

If your company matches employee contributions, you are doing even better. In addition to the tax reduction, you are also getting free money.

Many companies pay a 50 percent match, so that in the scenario above; the employer would put $2,000 into the retirement fund.

Even if you are afraid of the market and have your retirement fund in a low paying money market at just 2 percent, your return on your investment would be 52 percent.

Company Stock Options

Traditionally, stock option plans have been used as a way for companies to reward top management and key employees and link their interests with those of the company and other shareholders.

DEFINITION: A stock option gives an employee the right to buy a certain number of shares in the company at a fixed price for a certain number of years.

The price at which the option is provided is called the "grant" price and is often the market price at the time the options are granted. Employees who have been granted stock options hope that the share price will go up and that they will be able to "cash in" by exercising (purchasing) the stock at the lower grant price and then selling the stock at the current market price.

What are the advantages to participating in a stock option program?

- These plans are easy and convenient to set up and encourage saving and investing.

- Employees do not have to commit to a specific number of shares each pay period. They select a dollar amount or a percentage of paycheck, and during every purchase period a number of shares are purchased based on contributions.

IRAs

DEFINITION:	An Individual Retirement Account is a personal savings plan that allows you to contribute up to $4,000 a year ($5000 in 2008). If you are over 50, you may contribute $5,000 in order to "catch up" during 2007 (there will be no catch up as of 2008).

A traditional IRA grows tax deferred. You pay no taxes on the interest earned until you gradually withdraw the sum between the ages of 59 ½ and 70 ½. The sooner you open an IRA, the more money you will have for your retirement.

There are several types of IRAs: a traditional IRA, a Roth IRA, Keogh IRA, and IRA-SEP. Talk with a financial planner or a tax consultant to determine which is best for you. (You can also compare a traditional IRA to a Roth IRA in the Retirement Appendices.)

Be sure to check all the different IRA options. Some charge a yearly fee, and some charge transaction fees. Others charge both. It does not take many fees to eat up interest and, sometimes, principal.

The IRA Growth Chart below is an example of the earning possibility of an IRA investment (7 percent interest compounded annually):

IRA GROWTH CHART			
Value of Your IRA	After If You Contribute $500 /Year ($9.62 /Week	If You Contribute $1,000 /Year ($19.23 /Week	If You Contribute $2,000 /Year ($38.46 /Week
1 Year	$535	$1,070	$2,140
5 Years	$3,077	$6,153	$12,307
10 Years	$7,392	$14,784	$29,567
20 Years	$21,933	$43,856	$87,730
30 Years	$50,537	$101,073	$202,146
40 Years	$106,805	$213,609	$427,219

Retirement savings tops the list of financial goals for most

Americans. With longer life expectancies and often more active retirement living, most of today's workers will need to accumulate a sizeable nest egg to supplement their Social Security benefits, and few will have a traditional pension to rely on. The best time to get started is now.

Retirement Sources of Income

Besides your savings plans toward retirement, you need to look at other sources of retirement income.

1. Will you be eligible for social security benefits? Will they keep up with inflation? Will they still be available when you retire?

2. Does your employer have a pension plan and are you eligible?

3. Will you still work on retirement?

4. Do you have a home or other real estate?

5. Will you be receiving an inheritance?

All these questions come into play when determining retirement needs.

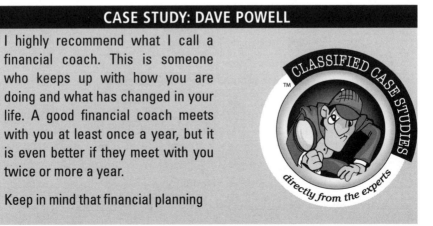

CASE STUDY: DAVE POWELL

I highly recommend what I call a financial coach. This is someone who keeps up with how you are doing and what has changed in your life. A good financial coach meets with you at least once a year, but it is even better if they meet with you twice or more a year.

Keep in mind that financial planning

CASE STUDY: DAVE POWELL

with a financial coach is a two-way street. If you tell your coach about financial and life circumstance changes, , then coaching will really work for you.

A good coach helps you determine a good financial plan based on your wants, needs, circumstances, and priorities. Sometimes the "normal" pattern is not the best avenue to take.

Financial planning is not a solid road map that never changes. You may have decided something at 21 that no longer fits into the scope of your life. These changes are often more complex than changing from a 401K to a self directed IRA.

Let us take a quick look at my own situation. When I turned 45, my wife found out that she was expecting twins – our first children. My desire was to be an involved dad. I could see myself in the backyard throwing a ball with my son. I could see myself going on vacation with my children and showing them great places like Disney World and the Grand Canyon. My plan to work until I was 62 or 65 and then retire did not seem to be the right plan anymore.

I knew that by the time I was 65, my kids would be grown and out of the house. They would have their own lives and the best that I could hope for was that I would live long enough for them to rediscover me when they got into their 20s.

So I decided to change my plan so that between ages 45 and 60, when my kids were younger, I would work less. At age 60, if I did not have enough to retire (and I probably will not), I would work more from age 60 to 70. When I retire at 70, they will be at the stage in their lives that they will rediscover me, and I will have a chance to be a part of their lives again. I had to change my financial plan to fit my circumstances, but more importantly, my priorities.

That is what a coach does for you as opposed to a financial planner. Coaches get to the core of your priorities and help you develop goals that meet those priorities. Planners may have a set formula. This formula may or may not work for you. A coach will help you see which parts of the formula work best for your situation and are adept at helping you through any life change to re-determine your goals.

CASE STUDY: DAVE POWELL

Before going through this experience, I had never met anyone who works this way. This is why I now work to guide clients based on their priorities and intelligent choices.

Another issue in financial planning is what I call caveman financing. Let us assume that you are a caveman who lives by a creek full of fish. In fact, there are one million fish in this creek. You can eat all the fish now and starve later, or you can save all the fish, having more than you can eat later and starve now. There is a middle line that is figured out with a budget and a strategy. It tells you what you can do to eat fish now and eat fish later. It establishes what you can do and where you are, and how much fun you can have and how much to save all based on your priorities and goals you set for yourself.

There are three phases of investment:

1. **The Accumulation Phase.** This is where you should save, save, save. In this phase the amount that you save far exceeds anything you can earn on those savings. The balance of your savings is so low that anywhere you put it (as long as it is exceeding inflation) is fine.

2. **The Management Phase.** When your earnings are more than you can possibly save, you have reached this phase. Here, the focus is on where to put it. You will make more money managing your funds than putting them into saving. This means that you will need to pick good investments and manage your risks wisely.

3. **The Retirement Phase.** The last phase is the retirement phase where you draw income off your investments. In this phase, all the prior rules concerning your portfolio no longer work. The average rate of return means nothing if there are down years and you are drawing off your portfolio interest.

Many financial planners suggest that people in the retirement phase should always take low risk. I say, yes and no. The risk you take in the retirement phase depends entirely upon your situation.

In retirement, you cannot draw more than 4.5 percent against a portfolio without running a substantial risk of running out of money after 20 to

CASE STUDY: DAVE POWELL

25 years. Those coming into retirement at this stage live longer than that. They tend to have 30 to 35 years in retirement. They need their retirement to work a lot longer for them than their grandparents did. Their grandparents could draw six percent to eight percent and not run out of money.

If you have a limited amount of retirement investments that need to see you through 35 years, you will have to make low risk decisions.

On the other hand, I have a couple that is living off $50,000 per year in interest from $2.5 million in investments. This amount of money in their small rural community, especially with no mortgage to pay, allows them to live quite comfortably. They could lose ½ of their principal and still be just fine. Someone in this situation can have more risk.

The key to being successful is knowing what you want, what you need, and how you plan to get there. Successful is defined entirely by you. A good financial coach will help you get to your definition of success.

Dave Powell and Associates

Ameriprise Financial Services, Inc

Dave Powell, CFP, CLU, CRPC

Senior Financial Advisor

284 West Millbrook Road

Raleigh, NC 27609

919-870-8930

david.r.powell@ampf.com

Social Security

The Social Security Administration expects that by 2040, the payroll taxes collected will only be enough to pay about 74 percent of scheduled benefits. That means if you expect $2,000 a month from social security, plan for $1500.

Your benefit depends on the age you retire and your contributions into the fund. Putting $66,000 into Social Security Tax with your employee paying an equal amount, your benefits would be:

- Retire at 62 $1,400/month
- Retire at 66 $1,800/month
- Retire at 70 $2,400/month

Waiting eight years makes a significant difference in your retirement.

Each year you receive a benefits statement from the Social Security Administration. If you have not received one, request one by visiting the Web site **www.ssa.gov** or by calling 800-772-1213.

Pensions

Very few pensions exist in today's world. Once, if you worked for a company until retirement, you could expect a pension that would take care of you during retirement. Most employers have turned to a 401(k) or a 403(b) plan. These plans leave everything up to the employee. You decide the amount put into the account and the way to invest the funds.

Reverse Mortgage

DEFINITION:	A reverse mortgage is a loan against the equity in a home.

A reverse mortgage provides tax-free cash advances to the

homeowner, but requires no payments during the term of the loan. The proceeds from a reverse mortgage are available as a lump sum; fixed monthly payments to you for as long as you live in your home; a line of credit; or a combination of these options.

These proceeds can be used for daily living expenses, home repairs and home improvements, medical bills and prescription drugs, pay-off of existing debts, education, travel, long-term health care, retirement and estate tax planning.

If you have an elderly parent who is in need of help and who owns a home, you may opt for reverse mortgage to increase the parent's cash flow without adding more expenses. With your own home, this might be a good way to supplement your retirement. You want to discuss these options with your lawyer, financial planner, or estate planner.

How Much Do You Need To Retire?

It depends on your current age, the age you wish to retire, how long you can reasonably expect to live after retirement, your current lifestyle, the lifestyle you expect to have on retirement, and other factors that will take a bit of work.

I would say that you would need 80 percent of your current income per year in retirement for each year that you are retired. For someone making $40,000 per year, you would need $32,000 per year. This money will come from a combination of all the sources I have already mentioned such as social security, savings, and current wages.

What is the reason for needing less than your current income? Your expenses will be reduced because you will no longer be paying Social Security taxes or making retirement plan contributions or spending money on job related expenses and disability insurance You may decide that life insurance is no longer worth the premiums. Your mortgage may be paid off. All these factors will reduce your monthly income needs.

Some expenses will increase:

- **Travel expenses** – you may want to travel around the country or the world and travel to see your children and grandchildren.

- **Medical care** – as you get older, your medical expenses will go up, even with Medicaid.

- **Long-term care** – insurance premiums or long-term care itself.

- **Hobbies** – these often become expensive in retirement because you finally have time to enjoy them.

If your retirement needs are $34,000 a year, multiply that by 25 for a yield of $850,000, the retirement savings at 4 percent needed to provide your annual income without touching your principal. Knowing you will be getting $20,000 in Social Security, you will now only need $14,000 annual income; multiplying that by 25 yields $350,000 retirement savings; still a large number, but much less than the original figure. If inflation is less or you earn more than four percent on your investments, the numbers go down even further.

Look in the Retirement Appendices for a worksheet that will help you determine how much to save per year in order to retire in style.

John had slippery hands – no money could stay in them. His advisor helped him with a budgeting plan and six months later, he called his advisor to tell him that his aunt had died and left him an inheritance. He needed help knowing what to do with it. When the advisor pulled into the yard, there sat two brand new cars. Not only that, but the house had all new furniture. This is not necessarily bad, but John did not have a plan.

The advisor suggested he look toward college for his two children and set aside this money in an investment that was difficult to get to. He also helped John do the same for retirement. Within six years, John exhausted the inheritance. Now he is in his 60s and saying to himself, if only I had done this or if only I had done that, I would have enough money for retirement.

When people get to this point without enough money for retirement, they finger point. The best thing would have been to make good choices in the beginning. Since John did not, he needs to find the right choices to make now.

With planning and forethought, you can have the retirement you wish to have. Retirement does not have to be difficult.

The next three chapters will teach you how to establish credit, avoid debt, and repair credit.

NOW YOU KNOW
1. Only 61 percent of those eligible participate in a 401(k) do so. Of those who do participate, many do not contribute the maximum allowed each year.
2. There are several types of IRAs including a traditional IRA, a Roth IRA, Keogh IRA, and an IRA-SEP. The best way to determine which is best for you is to talk with a financial planner or a tax consultant.
3. The Social Security Administration expects that by 2040, payroll taxes collected will be enough to pay only about 74 percent of scheduled benefits.
4. There are many sources of income for retirement including social security benefits, pensions, 401(k) and IRA withdrawals, investment income, and reverse mortgages.
5. Although there is no finite amount needed for retirement, generally you will need 80 percent of your current income per year for each year that you are retired.

CHAPTER 8:
Establishing Credit

Your finances, including credit, are built over time and should be properly maintained throughout the rest of your life. Patience pays off.

Unsecured and Secured Major Credit Cards

Obtaining a secured or unsecured major credit card is a first step in establishing credit.

DEFINITION:	An unsecured loan or credit card is one that does not require property as collateral. A secured loan requires collateral – property that will be seized if the loan is not paid.

The most common collateral for a credit card is a savings account. You are obligated to open a savings account with a deposit equal to the credit limit. Some banks give up to 50 percent more credit than the deposited amount.

After you have made on-time payments for six to twelve months, the bank will send your savings account deposit back with interest earned and convert your secured card to an unsecured account.

If you have been granted a low limit on your new card, do not go on a spending spree. Make small purchases to establish an on-time payment history. These low-limit credit card accounts will help you begin to build your credit.

Signature and Passbook Loans

Borrowing money and paying it back to a local bank is one of the most effective ways to build a payment history. Bank credit is best for building your credit and credit score.

How can you borrow money from a bank if you have no credit or bad credit? If you have $2,000, go to a bank (major national bank preferably) and open a basic savings account in your name or purchase a six-month Certificate of Deposit (CD). The following week go back to the same bank and ask the loan officer to help you obtain a $2,000 simple interest signature or passbook loan.

Have the loan payments set up for 12 to 24 months. The longer the repayment terms the lower your monthly payment. You will not be making payments for the entire length of the term anyway, so 24 months should be a good term that will make your monthly payments affordable.

The loan officer will process your application and pull your credit. He will ask for collateral for your $2000 loan. Let the loan officer know you wish to pledge your existing savings account or CD, as security for your loan. The loan officer will approve your secured loan, and issue you a payment coupon book. You will also receive a bank check for $2,000, the proceeds of your new loan.

Remember that your original $2,000 in your new savings account or CD is being used as collateral for your loan. The $2,000 you have in your hand is a loan.

Repeat this process. Locate a different bank—not just a different branch of the same bank above. Take the $2,000 in your hand (proceeds from the above loan) and open up another savings account or buy a six-month CD from them.

A week later go to the new bank and ask to borrow $2,000 using your savings account or CD as security for your loan. You will be given another payment coupon book and a bank check for $2,000.

The final bank loan can be used to pay the different loan payments that you have created. This will cost you the interest of the loan for three to six months, but it is an easy and effective way to establish credit.

During this six-month period, each bank will report your on-time payments to the three major credit bureaus. At the end of the six-month period, you will have established three new solid bank credit references. Just those three bank credit references will create a solid foundation on which to build an eventual "powerhouse" credit report.

After your six months of on time payments, many new credit opportunities will open up for you, from competitive automobile loans to mortgages. Lenders will seek you out. Remember that these offers of credit are not an open invitation to go wild with spending. The most important factor is controlling your debt.

At the end of six months, pay off your loans and close out your savings accounts. The bank will calculate your loan payoff, and then satisfy the outstanding balance with your $2000 savings account or CD. They will also give you credit for the interest you earned on your savings deposit or CD. The money left over will be given back to you.

Applying for Credit

Always be truthful and accurate when applying for credit. The items a lender pays the most attention to are:

- Time at current residence (longer is better)

- Annual or monthly income (higher is better)

- Length of employment (longer is better)

Applications will ask to list your debts. The lender will see these on your credit bureau reports. I would not list debts that do not show on your credit reports because the lender will see only the debt reported.

Verify the information on your credit report. Errors may lead to credit denial.

Multiple credit applications — applying for too much credit at one time — will put up a red flag with creditors. Too many credit inquiries will lower your credit score. Apply for credit that is needed — not everything you want.

Sometimes you may not have control of how many people pull your credit report. Car dealers like to send your application to a dozen or more banks and finance companies to make sure you get financed. Each one of these lenders may pull a credit report or two on you. This practice hurts your credit. Ask the dealer to submit to just a few banks. Better yet, obtain your own financing before you go shopping.

Personal Financial Statements

DEFINITION: A financial statement is a listing of your assets and liabilities.

Rarely, will you need a prepared financial statement to obtain basic consumer credit.

One instance is if you are self-employed. Lenders will require your W-2s and tax returns, depending on your type of purchase and condition of your credit.

Cosigners

A fast way to get credit is having a friend or family member co-sign for a credit card, auto loan, or a mortgage.

DEFINITION:	A cosigner is an individual who makes an agreement to guarantee your repayment of a debt.

The cosigner must have good credit, and be willing to take a financial risk when endorsing your obligation. With the loan or credit card in place, your creditor will begin to report your account to the national credit bureaus. This joint account will show up on your cosigner's credit reports, too. Late payments on joint accounts will reflect poorly on your cosigner's credit report, too. After 12 to 24 months of timely payments the lender may take your cosigner off your loan.

Good credit is valuable since having it gives you the ability to borrow funds to buy things that might take years and years to afford, like a home or college education. This makes credit a good financial tool. However, like most tools, it can be abused and dangerous. That is why learning how to use credit wisely is one of the most valuable financial skills anyone can learn.

In the next chapters you will learn how to avoid debt and how to get out of debt if you have already had money problems.

NOW YOU KNOW
1. Bank credit is best for building your credit and credit score.
2. With loan or credit card applications, being truthful and accurate is most important.
3. Do not make multiple credit applications at one time. This kind of activity throws a red flag to creditors. Too many creditor inquiries will lower your credit score. Apply for what you need, not for everything you want.
4. A fast way to get your credit going in the right direction is to have a friend or family member co-sign for a credit card, auto loan, or a mortgage.

CHAPTER 9:
Avoiding Debt and Bankruptcy

Good Debt Versus Bad Debt

Financial advisors agree that some debts are acceptable. Mortgage and educational loans are considered good debts because:

1. They are investing in your future and will pay you back either through equity or increased pay.

2. The interest rates are low and can be written off.

Bankers will assure you that there is a particular percentage of debt to income that is acceptable. Do not listen. They want you to have as much debt as possible without going bankrupt so that they will make money on your interest. Banks will suggest that you can have up to a 40 percent debt to income ratio. The truth is 15 percent is the most you should go above your mortgage or educational loans. You can learn to figure out your debt to income ratio by using the formula found in the Debt Appendices.

How to Tell if You Are In Over Your Head

Credit is good when it is used wisely, but more Americans are getting in over their heads and threatening their financial futures. Paying minimum payments each month leads to credit problems. Low minimum payments benefit the credit card company, not you. They enslave you to your debt, taking decades to pay off purchases whose prices become inflated by interest charges.

Do not be lulled into the false sense of security that your debt is under control just because you are not late on any payments and you manage to pay the monthly minimums.

Entertainment on Credit: Not a Good Idea

Do not use your credit card to purchase items that lose value quickly—food, drinks, and entertainment—unless you plan to pay off the balance each month.

There are times where buying something on a credit card is necessary. For instance, I needed a new voice recorder and multidirectional microphone in order to write this book. I used my credit card because I simply did not have the cash available at the moment. Luckily for me, I delved into my emergency funds and paid it off the first month without having to pay any interest. If you do not yet have an emergency account, plan to pay off such a purchase as quickly as possible.

Avoid Credit Cards To Avoid Credit Card Debt

You do not need:

- More than two major credit cards

- High credit limits

Steel yourself against the temptation to spend. There are three credit-reporting bureaus in the United States. Write a letter to each one of them, asking to be removed from any unsolicited mailings offering credit cards. You can call an 800 number to be removed, for two years, from all three companies. (See the Debt Appendix.)

CASE STUDY: MEG G.

The biggest mistake we made financially was to use credit cards. We justified our wants as needs and made them happen with plastic. An example is charging $300 worth of groceries when we knew we could only afford to spend $40 that week.

We also cared too much about our image. We needed to get every family member, 45 in all, a nice Christmas and birthday gift. We had to have a new car and things to make us look good to everyone.

Those were not the only issues. We also made a budget that we never followed,. did not make saving a priority, lived for the "now" instead of the "what if", and did not want to face the bad things that could happen like sick children or a job loss, so that when they did happen, we had no contingency plan. We skipped a payment here to make a payment there from month to month.

My husband lost his job three times in a two year span. We went through his small severances just keeping our heads above water. I could not pay for my child's prescription. I would beg the pharmacist to dispense the medication in smaller amounts.

My son was very sick and I had to humble myself by calling his doctor to admit that I did not have enough money to pay for an appointment or medication. I did not have enough money to take my children to the dentist. When I was pregnant, I had to decide between proper prenatal care and buying an older child new glasses.

Our phone and water were turned off, and I had to ask a relative to pay our power bill. We plummeted to our financial nadir the day I had to go to a food bank. Enough was enough; we could not live like this anymore.

CASE STUDY: MEG G.

We contacted Consumer Credit Counseling (CCC). That program did not work for us. The payment expected was more than we could afford and covered only some of the money we owed. We could not include all our creditors or the payment would have been more than our mortgage. Several creditors refused the program. We were late on our mortgage payments just to pay CCC. We decided to file bankruptcy but we did not even have enough money for that. Plus, with the new laws, we would have had to go into a repayment program that we could not afford. We attempted to take a home equity loan, but when my husband lost his job, the bank withdrew the loan.

We had no choice but to put our home on the market and use the profit to pay off all our debts and sustain us through the job search.

Starting the CCC process was the first step in fixing our debt problem. It forced us to organize our finances and debts and face where we were. The second step was growing up and realizing that we got ourselves into this mess. Our situation had very little to do with the job loss.

We needed to think before buying. We needed to separate needs from wants and then get a second opinion. We needed to think cash first, and most of all, we needed to say no.

We had to reeducate our children and ourselves. I attended Debtors Anonymous meetings. We explained our goals to our children in a way that would not worry them and asked for their cooperation by not asking for things they did not need.

The hardest step was growing up. We could have gotten by borrowing money from our family. We could have stayed on the same track and lived in the house until the police had to drag us out. We could have kept assigning blame and spent our time angry at his former workplace. We wanted to do those things and, for a while, we did.

I think accepting personal responsibility is the most crucial step there is. We are not what happens to us. We are how we prepare and deal with what happens to us. If we do not accept responsibility, we will continue through life on the same track and we will teach our children to do the same.

At this point, I would rate us as solidly recovering. We are debt free.

The Truth Behind Minimum Payments

The minimum monthly payment on most credit cards is calculated as a certain percentage (often around two percent) of your total balance.

On a $1,000 TV, two percent of the balance is $20. At 18 percent interest, your $20 payment will include $15 in interest and only $5 toward the amount you borrowed (18 percent divided by 360 days = .05 percent per day times 30 days in a month times $1,000 outstanding balance equals $15 in interest). If you pay the minimum balance each month it will take you more than 30 years to pay off your $1,000 TV. You will pay nearly $2,500 in interest. The $1,000 TV will cost nearly $3,500. By putting that same $20 a month into an investment account that earns 8 percent for the same number of years (30). Your $20 a month would be worth over $20,000.

Educate yourself about the true cost of credit. Credit has its place, but using it unwisely can cripple you financially.

Avoiding College Tuition Debt Through Financial Aid

College aid can come from a variety of federal or state agencies, private lending institutions, or through scholarships from your employer, church, club, or even the college your child wishes to attend.

The federal government provides the majority of financial aid — about 66 percent annually. More than $94 billion in federal student aid was handed out for the 2005-06 school year, according to the College Board.

Federal aid includes loans, grants, and campus-based programs and is based on financial need rather than scholastic achievement. There are three types of loans: Stafford student loans, PLUS loans for parents and Perkins loans for high financial need students.

The Federal Pell Grant that does not have to be repaid is awarded to undergraduate students based on financial need, cost of attendance, and other factors. For students who are Pell Grant-eligible, the government introduced two new grants in 2006: the Academic Competitiveness Grant and the National SMART Grant.

Campus-based programs like work-study let students earn money to pay for school. To receive any form of aid, students must fill out the Free Application for Federal Student Aid (FAFSA) online at **www.fafsa.ed.gov.**

DEFINITION: The FAFSA is the first application to be completed to apply for all types of financial aid for higher education. This form is distributed and processed by the U.S. Department of Education.

The Internet application can be completed until July 2, 2007.

Filling out the form can be confusing, but having your completed tax returns and year-end statements detailing your investments will ease the confusion. The application will take about one hour.

Financial aid is based on your family's expected contribution. The less you can contribute, the more likely your child will receive aid. On these forms, your retirement account or home does not have to be put down as assets.

Read the directions and do not skip any questions. Each question is designed to find out how much aid your child should receive. Failing to or incorrectly answering a question can mean the difference between getting a federal grant for college and having to pay for it yourself.

Two to four weeks after submitting the FAFSA, you will receive a Student Aid Report.

DEFINITION:	A Student Aid Report summarizes the information you reported on the FAFSA and tells you your Estimated Family Contribution (EFC).

Financial aid administrators at the colleges where you have applied use your EFC to determine how much aid you get. You will receive an award letter explaining the amount of aid being awarded you for the school year and in what form: loan, grant, campus-based program, or a combination of the three. The letter will tell you what steps to take next.

If you are not eligible for financial aid, junior or community college is an option. Check whether the four-year institution you would like to attend will allow transfer of credits from your two-year colleges when you enroll as a junior. (If a counselor at the two-year school assures you that your credits will transfer, get the statement in writing.) The savings in tuition costs can be 40 to 45 percent.

Avoiding Car Loan Debt

Get yourself an older car that is mechanically safe and has airbags, paying with cash. Instead of paying $200 a month in car payments, you can put $200 a month toward long-term savings goals, realizing your financial goals.

Rules for Avoiding Debt

Some common-sense rules can help you avoid debt:

- Cash, not credit, for purchases.

- Know and keep your budget.

- Do not buy something that costs more than $10 without thinking it through.

- Compare prices before making major purchases.

- Do not try to keep up with the Joneses.

- When shopping, take only the cash you will need.

- Do not use a credit card for food.

- If you borrow money, find the lowest possible interest rate.

- Do not overdraw your checking – fees are costly.

- Always pay more than the minimum payment on credit card bills.

- Never have more than two major credit cards.

- Take yourself off the mailing lists of the credit reporting bureaus to stop credit card solicitations if you cannot resist the temptation to sign up.

What To Do If You Already Have Debt

Pay it off.
Get rid of the cards: Cut up the credit cards. Stop charging new money to them.

Pay down the debt. Start with the loan or credit card that has the highest interest.

Get your interest reduced: Pressure your credit card company to lower your interest rate with the threat of transferring your balance to another company.

Use extra money to pay off debt: Investing money instead of paying off debt is a bad idea. There are not many investments that earn more than credit card interest costs.

Investing $1,000 instead of paying off credit card debt will yield $2,300 in interest in 10 years; credit card debt of $1,000 will cost $4,900 in interest over 10 years.

Debt and Divorce

In divorce, couples often have more debts to split up than assets. The problem is figuring out how to divide up the debts.

In most states, debts prior to marriage belong to that individual. Any debts that incurred during the marriage are shared by the couple. The problem is not all states treat debt the same.

Sometimes one partner will trade some debt for more equity in a house or a retirement plan. If there is $10,000 in debt, the partner with the higher earnings may agree to assume 70 percent of the debt to get 70 percent of the retirement plan. For agreements that are not typical of state laws, be sure to have papers drawn up by a lawyer. Without these papers, your credit rating can still be attached to the debt and you may also be legally bound to pay if your partner does not.

You want to close out any joint accounts. If a credit card with $4,000 worth of debt is in both names, the card should be closed out and the balance transferred to a new card with only the name of the partner responsible for that particular debt. Freeze any joint account so that no new debts may be made. The best way to handle joint debt is to pay it off before the divorce is final. This is done by selling off joint property or borrowing your portion of the debt from a bank or family member. Get everything in writing and make it legal.

Avoid Debt Repair Scams

DEFINITION: A debt repair scam is a false promise to fix your credit by requiring upfront fees.

Scam companies appeal to consumers with poor credit histories, promising that they will clean up bad credit reports for a fee. They leave the consumer with fewer resources and more delinquent debt.

Tips to avoid scams:

- Beware of promises that sound too good to be true.

- Deal with a reputable agency by checking with state consumer agencies and the local Better Business Bureau.

- Non-profit credit counseling organizations are the best choices.

- Verify that the organization provides counseling and education, debt consolidation, and payment services.

- Carefully read through the agreement the credit counseling organization offers.

- Avoid paying upfront fees.

- Beware of any high fees or required contributions, like high monthly service charges that add to the debt load and defeat efforts to pay off bills.

- Confirm payments with creditors.

NOW YOU KNOW
1. Making minimum credit card payments each month is a credit problem.
2. Buying food, drinks, and entertainment with a credit card without paying off the balance each month makes no sense.
3. The minimum monthly payment on credit cards is calculated as a percentage (often around two percent) of your total balance.

CHAPTER 10:
Fixing Your Credit

The First Step

Find out what is being reported about you. Doing so is easy and inexpensive.

DEFINITION:	A consumer credit report is a record of your credit activities. It reports all your credit accounts and outstanding loans, the balances on your credit cards and loans, and your bill paying history.

For under $10, you can get your credit report from one of the three main credit-reporting companies:

- **Equifax at www.equifax.com or 1-800-997-2493**

- **Experian at www.experian.com or 1-800-397-3742**

- **TransUnion at www.transunion.com or 1-800-888-4213**

You can get a free credit report from each major credit bureau if you:

- Have been denied credit in the last 60 days.

- Are unemployed and plan on seeking employment in the next 60 days.

- Are on public welfare assistance.

- Suspect that there has been fraudulent activity involving your personal credit.

Also, a new program allows U.S. residents to get one free credit report per year.

For a copy of your free credit report, call 1-877-322-8228 or visit **www.annualcreditreport.com.** Request by mail at: Annual Credit Report Request Service, P.O. Box 105281, Atlanta, GA 30348-5281.

After You Receive Your Report

Each credit bureau will enclose instructions on how to read your credit report and one blank form used to dispute inaccurate and obsolete account information.

Highlight every account that is reporting negative, incorrect, or obsolete information. Fill out the account information requested — on each dispute form.

Note: Use the right dispute form for each individual credit bureau report. Use certified mail to keep track which agency and person you wrote, when you wrote, and who received the mail on the credit bureau's end. Ask the credit bureau to send a corrected report to anyone who has requested a report on you in the last six months. The credit bureaus will update your credit files and place a statement next to each account that you are disputing.

Each credit bureau will then send a notice or "request for updated account information" to each creditor whose reported account you are disputing. This notice will ask each creditor to update your account information and to verify that the account is yours. Each credit bureau has 30 days in which to send out your dispute and receive a reply from the creditors they contacted on your behalf.

If the credit bureaus do not receive a reply within about 30 days, by law they must completely delete the negative account from your credit bureau report. They are often prohibited from re-reporting deleted accounts after the 30 day response period.

Talk to Those You Owe

Creditors want their money. They do not want you to default. Most creditors will work with you to get a reduced payment schedule. If you can keep them from reporting you to the credit bureau, it will not hurt your credit. Stick to the negotiated plan: they will not renegotiate if you fail to comply.

If they have already reported you to the credit bureau, you want to negotiate with them to remove the bad item. Offer a settlement in exchange for the complete removal of the item from your credit report. The creditor may say yes or make you a counter offer. If their counter offer is acceptable or they say yes, have them send you a settlement agreement.

Sometimes creditors want a full payment of the balance in exchange for the removal of your account from your credit files. Try to get them to take a discount first. If it is a large balance, offer to make payments until it is satisfied, and then have them remove the account from your national credit bureaus records. Whichever way you structure it, get it in writing that they agree to permanently remove the account from your credit files after it is paid.

In the event they refuse to remove the account, make sure they agree in writing to report a zero balance within 30 days of being paid. While the account will still show on your credit file, a zero balance reported is much better than debt still showing owed.

This Could Be You

CASE STUDY: ANGELA A. ADAMS

My mistake was applying for credit cards and using them right away for things that were not lasting or necessary. I did not pay them off each month. I compounded my mistake by spending any extra money I had instead of paying off bills. I was in college and thought I had plenty of time to do so.

While in college, I got married. We settled into married housing on campus. I did not pay attention to our housing costs because they were put on my school bill, another bill I did not take care of.

I am now divorced and paying off those loans – all $35,000 worth. I could have prevented $15,000 of this debt by paying the rent.

I did not realize I was in financial trouble until we had to get a loan to help pay off other bills. That was my light bulb. I tried to manage all the bills the best I could, but my ex-husband kept quitting his jobs and the past due fees kept rolling in. Because the credit cards were maxed out, the credit card companies started charging over-the-limit fees.

We had 12 credit cards. Nine of them were in my name. We separated after I graduated. He would not help make payments, and I was stuck with the debt. I could not take care of all the bills myself and just about let them all go.

I knew I could not pay off all the cards and the regular bills, too. So, I went online and started searching for credit help. I found American Consumer Credit Counseling (ACCC). I enrolled in their debt management plan. They contacted all the credit companies and got them to lower their interest rates, take away some of the fees they had charged, and stop charging additional fees. They got me a reasonable payment each month and a portion of it went to each card.

I moved, got a new job, and worked on paying off the debt with

CASE STUDY: ANGELA A. ADAMS

ACCC helping. I have been in the program two years and have five cards paid off.

I do not apply for credit or purchase anything on credit. I maintain a very strict budget. If I do not have it, I do not spend it.

I am attempting to pay ACCC off early. I am paying $258 a month. Instead of three and a half years total, I hope to have it paid off by the end of the year. That would put me at two and a half years in the program. I also completed a money management course through ACCC, receiving a certificate and a note sent to all three credit reporting agencies.

The hardest part of all this was admitting that I could not pay this all off without some kind of help. After I realized I needed the help, I had to tell them each card and each amount. It was embarrassing. After the embarrassment was over, I realized how hard it was going to be — and it has been. I pay $258 a month toward paying off the almost $14,000 in credit card debt I had. That is humiliating.

Admitting that I was in trouble was huge. If you do not think you have a problem, it is never going to get better. I may have paid off the debt myself, but in the future I would have ended up going right back to it.

I have come a long way. I had a 493 credit score a year ago; now, it is 583. I am still not where I want to be. I am still paying for my careless spending, but I am working myself out of it. I am proud of how far I have come.

Judgments

Judgments showing on your credit reports will not come off for ten years or more depending on your state's statute of limitations. However, a zero balance looks better on your report than money owed. Get a Satisfaction of Judgment from the judgment holder when the debt is paid. Record the Satisfaction of Judgment in your county's official public records. Keep copies of the recorded satisfaction to prove to future creditors the debt was paid. Credit bureaus tend to not update their files in a timely manner. Send the reporting credit bureau a copy of the satisfaction to speed them along.

Consumer Statement

DEFINITION: A consumer statement is a 100 word personal explanation made by you that is added to each of your credit reports.

Writing a consumer statement can increase your credit score. Explain the reasons you have negative accounts on your credit reports: job loss, medical problems, divorce. By submitting this statement, you look more responsible to future lenders. Creditors understand that bad events happen to people.

What You Do Not Need

You do not need a repair clinic. There is no legal way to repair your debt. Those that claim to know loopholes and shortcuts are merely out for your money. They may even get you into legal trouble by having you fudge facts or by creating a whole new file for you. Anything legal that a clinic can do, you can do just as easily and without the cost of professional help.

Chapter Eleven takes you from looking at houses to the closing meeting.

NOW YOU KNOW
1. Borrowers must have self-control over their spending practices.
2. Your credit reports can have old, obsolete, and incorrect information. Dispute these discrepancies.
3. Most creditors will work with you to get a reduced payment schedule.
4. By law, you are allowed to add information to your report that will help your rating.
5. You do not need a repair clinic. There is no legal way to repair your credit quickly.

CHAPTER 11:
Buying a Home

<table>
<tr><td>**DEFINITION:**</td><td>A down payment is money you pay to the bank when you take out a loan. The amount for a mortgage is usually 3 percent to 20 percent of the price of the house.</td></tr>
</table>

The size of the down payment you make on a mortgage loan depends on your credit and your mortgage type.

<table>
<tr><td>**DEFINITION:**</td><td>A conventional loan is any kind of lender agreement that is not backed in full by the Veterans Administration (VA) or protected by the Federal Housing Administration (FHA). Since the government does not back it, this loan has tougher approval standards.</td></tr>
</table>

Conventional Loan: With a conventional loan, the bank expects five percent to twenty percent down.

<table>
<tr><td>**DEFINITION:**</td><td>The FHA loan guarantees that a lender will not have to write off a loan if the borrower defaults. The FHA will pay. Because of this guarantee, lenders are willing to make large mortgage loans.</td></tr>
</table>

FHA: First-time home buyers might qualify for an FHA loan, and put three percent to five percent down. The loan is made by the bank. FHA guarantees part of the loan.

FHA loans are easier to get than conventional loans if you have credit problems. Not all sellers will agree to an FHA loan because there is more red tape involved, and the house must be in excellent shape to pass an FHA inspection.

DEFINITION:	Banks and other private mortgage companies make a special type of home loan to veterans of the U.S. Armed Services. A portion of each loan is guaranteed by the VA and protects the lender's investment if the borrower defaults.

VA: Like FHA loans, the VA does not lend money; it just guarantees part of the loan. Qualified veterans can get loans up to $203,000 with no down payment.

How Much Home Is Enough?

Banks suggest that you can afford a home that is three times your annual income: $50,000 annual income equals a $150,000 home.

Financial advisors suggest an affordable home is two and a half times annual income: $50,000 income equals $125,000 home.

Here are some factors to consider when determining the size of your loan:

- The higher your debt, the lower your mortgage should be.

- A large down payment enables you to increase loan size.

- Good credit can mean lower mortgage rates.

Qualifying For A Mortgage

Banks do not loan money to everyone who asks. They want to feel secure that the borrower is able and responsible enough to pay them back. You need four things to qualify for a mortgage:

1. Money to make the down payment

2. Income that is two to three times higher than your mortgage payment

3. Two years of solid employment history

4. Good credit

Never assume you cannot get a mortgage. Talk to a bank to see where your deficiencies are and work toward qualifying in the future.

Try to get a Low-Doc or No-Doc Loan. In recent years, banks have been offering loans to people who cannot, or do not want to, provide details about their income or their employment. The most popular is the "stated income" loan because you just "state" how much income you have without offering any proof. It is also called NIV for "No Income Verification."

Since the bank is taking a bigger risk on you with a No-Doc or Low-Doc loan, the interest rate is higher than on a traditional loan, and the exact amount depends on your credit score, your lender's preference, and which type of low-doc/no-doc loan you get. The premium you will pay will range from 0.125 to 3.0 percentage points over a traditional loan.

Also consider using a mortgage broker. Brokers charge a fee for this service but if you cannot get a mortgage otherwise, it could be worth it.

DEFINITION: A mortgage broker represents many different lenders and can shop around to try to find one who will offer you a loan.

You might also try to get the owner to finance all or part of the cost of the home. Getting an owner to finance a home is difficult, but with no other options, it is worth a try. You can increase your chances of success by offering to pay a higher interest rate.

Finally, consider a cosigner. See if a family member or friend with a higher income and better credit than yours will cosign a loan for you.

If you cannot buy a home now, making home-owning a serious goal can overcome most or all the obstacles above.

Understanding Closing Costs

In addition to the down payment, you will also have to pay closing costs.

DEFINITION: Closing costs are miscellaneous fees charged by your lender for processing the loan, the title company for handling the paperwork, a surveyor, local government offices for recording the deed, and others depending on laws in your state.

Closing costs vary. The range is from 1 percent to 8 percent of the price of the home, though more often 2 percent to 3 percent. These costs are significant.

Your lender can give a good faith estimate of closing costs on the house you have selected.

If you do not have enough cash for the closing costs, you can get the closing costs added to the amount of the loan. If the loan amount is for $150,000, and the closing costs are $4500, by adding the closing costs you would be borrowing $154,500 total.

DEFINITION:	The LTV is the amount of the loan compared to the value of the house, based on the appraisal.

For instance, a house is worth $100,000, and the bank will loan up to a 95 percent LTV, $95,000. If your credit is bad, the bank might only loan up to an 80 percent LTV, $80,000.

Do not confuse the price of the house with the value of the house. The bank gets the value of the house from the appraiser. The selling price could be higher or lower than the appraised value.

If you cannot roll the closing costs into the mortgage, see if the seller is willing to pay part of the closing costs. Some lenders will pay part or all the closing costs, but in exchange you will have to pay a higher interest rate on the loan, perhaps 0.25 percent or 0.50 percent higher. Ask your lender if this is an option.

Get Pre-qualified

DEFINITION:	Pre-qualification is a discussion between a home buyer and a loan officer regarding the buyer's basic information such as income, monthly debts, credit history, and assets to calculate an estimated mortgage amount that the home buyer can afford. A pre-qualification is not a full mortgage approval.

By getting pre-qualified, you are finding a bank willing to give you a loan. So how do you find a lender? Go to the bank that holds your checking or savings account. Try an online lender. Try a local mortgage broker. A mortgage broker works with dozens of different lenders.

To be pre-qualified, you will need to fill out a loan application that asks about your financial status and employment history. You will also have to provide a paycheck stub and your income tax return. Filling out an application does not obligate you to buy a house or accept a loan.

Lenders charge you $40 or more to run a credit check. After they have processed your application and run your credit report, they will to tell you how much they are willing to lend and under what circumstances.

If you are going to rent out part of your new home then that increases your income, and the bank will give you a bigger loan. If you are buying a duplex or a house with a garage apartment, ask the lender how much extra you can borrow, given the typical income you would expect to make from rent.

Shop for a loan like you shop for anything else, by considering the cost and by comparing what you get. The cost is the interest rate you will be paying on the note, plus any fees the bank charges. Interest rates and fees vary from lender to lender. You should always get an offer from at least:

- Two banks, or

- Two brokers, or

- A bank and a broker

If your lender or broker knows you are not talking to anyone else, what incentive do they have to give you the best deal? None. And you will pay more.

You should let the parties know they have competition. If you just accept the better offer, you will miss the opportunity to negotiate an even better deal., "Another broker or lender is offering 6 percent. Can you tell me why I should take your loan instead?" At that point he might lower his rate to 6 percent. You might not get a better deal, but it is worth asking.

After the bank has processed your application and run your credit report, they know how much they are willing to loan you.

After you qualify for a loan, the lender can give you a Pre-Qualification

Letter. Ask each lender for this letter. It shows real estate agents and sellers that you are serious about buying a house.

Types of Mortgage Offers You May Receive

The bank will offer three different mortgage options.

Fixed Rate versus Adjustable Rate Mortgages

DEFINITION:	If the interest rate stays the same over the life of the mortgage, this is called a fixed-rate mortgage (FRM). An Adjustable Rate Mortgage (ARM) has an interest rate that adjusts on a periodic basis, such as yearly or every two years.

Should you take the FRM or the ARM? The details in ARM offers are varied and hard to analyze. The general rule of thumb is, take the FRM unless the rate is above ten percent.

Read the fine print on an ARM offer. Pay an independent financial advisor $50 to evaluate the offer.

Origination Points

Most banks charge a fee to give a loan called the Origination Fee. They are charging money for the right to charge more money! The fee is a certain number of points.

DEFINITION:	A point is one percent of the purchase price of the home.

Buying a $100,000 home with the lender's charging two points will cost you $2,000. This amount is usually the biggest part. You can have this amount added to your loan amount instead of paying cash at closing.

Different banks charge different amounts of origination points, or nothing at all—this is something to consider when you are shopping around for a loan.

Discount Points

Banks will offer you a certain interest rate, but will let you buy the right to an even lower interest if you pay points. They might offer you a rate of seven percent but tell you that you can have a rate of 6.5 percent if you pay four points (four percent of the purchase price of the house). Which is the better deal? It depends on the effective interest rate.

Effective interest rate based on the number of points											
30-year mortgage											
Points	6%	6.5%	7%	7.5%	8%	8.5%	9%	9.5%	10%	10.5%	11%
1	6.09	6.60	7.10	7.60	8.10	8.61	9.11	9.62	10.12	10.62	11.13
2	6.19	6.69	7.20	7.70	8.21	8.72	9.22	9.73	10.24	10.74	11.25
3	6.28	6.79	7.30	7.80	8.31	8.82	9.33	9.84	10.35	10.87	11.38
4	6.38	6.88	7.39	7.91	8.42	8.93	9.44	9.96	10.47	10.99	11.50
5	6.46	6.98	7.49	8.01	8.52	9.04	9.55	10.07	10.59	11.11	11.63
6	6.55	7.07	7.59	8.11	8.62	9.14	9.66	10.19	10.71	11.23	11.75
7	6.64	7.16	7.68	8.21	8.73	9.25	9.77	10.30	10.82	11.35	11.87
8	6.73	7.26	7.78	8.31	8.83	9.36	9.88	10.41	10.94	11.47	12
30-year mortgage											
Points	6%	6.5%	7%	7.5%	8%	8.5%	9%	9.5%	10%	10.5%	11%
1	6.16	6.66	7.16	7.66	8.17	8.67	9.17	9.67	10.18	10.68	11.18
2	6.31	6.82	7.32	7.82	8.33	8.83	9.34	9.84	10.35	10.87	11.36
3	6.46	6.97	7.48	7.99	8.49	9.0	9.51	10.02	10.52	11.03	11.54
4	6.62	7.13	7.64	8.15	8.66	9.17	9.68	10.19	10.70	11.21	11.72
5	6.77	7.28	7.79	8.31	8.82	9.33	9.84	10.36	10.87	11.38	11.90

6	6.92	7.44	7.95	8.46	8.98	9.49	10.01	10.52	11.05	11.56	12.07
7	7.07	7.59	8.11	8.62	9.14	9.66	10.17	10.69	11.21	11.73	12.25
8	7.22	7.74	8.26	8.78	9.30	9.82	10.34	10.86	11.39	11.90	12.42

By looking at this table, you see that a rate of 6.5 percent with four points is just like a rate of 6.88 percent with no points. Since a 6.88 percent is better than seven percent, you want to pay for the lower interest rate.

If the bank offers you 6.6 percent with no points, or 6.5 percent with two points, the tables turn: 6.5 percent with two points is actually 6.69 percent, which is higher than the original offer of 6.6 percent. It is better to take the higher rate without points. You do not have to make your decision about which bank or broker to go with right now; save that for when you know which house you want to buy.

Benefits of Using a Real Estate Agent

There is no downside to using a real estate agent because the seller, not you, pays the agent's fees. Real estate agents have access to MLS, a database of all houses for sale that are listed by other real estate agents. Your real estate agent can find all the houses in MLS that match your needs. The real estate agent's ability to search MLS for you is less an advantage than it used to be, since it is now easy to find homes for sale on the Internet. You will also find FSBOs on the Internet.

DEFINITION: FSBOs, or For Sale By Owners, are sellers who put their home on the market without using a real estate agent. Doing so saves on commissions.

Real estate agents shy away from FSBOs for two reasons:

1. FSBOS are not listed in MLS.

2. Real estate agents make little or no commission on an FSBO.

If you find a home on your own, you can determine the value by going online and comparing recently sold properties near the home, or you may hire a real estate agent to perform a competitive market analysis (CMA) of the property to find its true value. The cost of a CMA is about $50.

DEFINITION: A CMA compares the house to similar houses in the neighborhood that have sold recently.

Another alternative to getting a CMA from a real estate agent is hiring an appraiser to provide you with an estimate of value. The appraisal will be much more detailed and more accurate than a real estate agent's market analysis, but it will cost more, $400 and up.

Is there any advantage to not using a real estate agent? The seller pays your real estate agent three percent of the purchase price. If you find the house yourself then the seller will not have to pay that three percent commission, and you might be able to convince the seller to lower the price by one percent, two percent, or even the full three percent. Most real estate agents will not tell you about houses that are For Sale By Owner (FSBO). A FSBO seller may still pay the three percent commission to the buyer's real estate agent, to get real estate agents to tell their buyers about the property. So the advantage of not using a real estate agent is a lower price from the seller.

Making an Offer

Making the offer does not obligate you to buy a house, especially if the inspection turns up physical problems with the structure. Your real estate agent can give you guidance about how much to offer. However, the real estate agent has two incentives to inflate the price. First, the higher the sales price, the more the agent's commission. Second, the more you offer, the more likely the seller will accept your offer.

You want to offer a lower price than the real estate agent suggested.

Before making an offer consider:

1. **The advice of your real estate agent** who is more familiar with the market and the process than you are. Even though the agent has a vested interest in the price's being higher, carefully consider what he or she tells you.

2. **How much will the bank loan you?** You can only go as high as the bank will loan.

3. **How much is the house worth?** We all want to avoid paying more than something is worth, and this is especially true when buying a house that you might want to sell someday.

4. **How much do you want the house?** There is nothing wrong with paying more than a house is worth if you really want the house and you can afford it.

The Contract

The way you make an offer is by signing a contract and paying earnest money—a small deposit. If the seller accepts your offer and signs the contract, you can proceed with the house inspection and appraisal. If he or she does not accept the offer, he or she can make a counter-offer. The process repeats until you have a contract signed by both parties. When the seller accepts your contract, he or she will take the house off the market. This secures your position as first in line to buy the house.

The seller's real estate agent will likely use the standard contract used in your state. You can find a sample of a Georgia contract in the Buying a Home Appendices. If the seller has written his own contract, have your real estate agent or an attorney look at it to make sure there is nothing disadvantageous to you in it.

Protection Against Buying a Lemon

Many standard state contracts say that the buyer can back out if lender-required repairs exceed five percent of the purchase price. Your lender does not want to lend money on a building that is in bad condition and may require that certain things be fixed. You will also choose one of two options on the contract to protect you:

1. An Option Fee ($100 +) that gives you the right to walk away for any reason.

Indicate in the contract that the seller will make repairs.

Option Fee. By paying an option fee directly to the seller, you get the right to walk away from the deal for any reason, within a certain time (often five days to two weeks). This allows you to get out of the contract if the inspection shows that the house is in much worse condition than you thought. If you do buy the house, the Option Fee is often applied toward the purchase. (Make sure that box is checked on the contract.) The option period is short, so if you do not want the house, do not delay in giving written notice that you want out, otherwise you will be stuck buying the house.

Seller-made Repairs. If you do not pay an option fee, you will want to write into the contract which repairs you want the seller to agree to make. The catch is that you will not know what repairs need to be made at the time you sign the contract because you have not had the inspection done yet. You might get the seller to agree to repair "any individual item found on the inspection which would cost $500 or more to be repaired by a licensed contractor." The seller is not obligated to agree to your proposal.

Earnest Money

DEFINITION:	Earnest money is a deposit you make when you make an offer on a house.

Earnest money is applied toward the purchase price if the deal goes through. If the deal does not go through, you can often get your earnest money back, though it depends on how the contract is worded. If you default on the contract, you can lose the earnest money.

After you sign the contract, make sure to have the inspection, survey, and appraisal performed quickly, or you can lose your earnest money.

After you have signed the contract and paid the earnest money, you will hire a professional inspection company to examine all the house's structural systems thoroughly and give you a written report detailing any problems found. Their fee will be $250 or more depending on the size of the home. You can find inspectors in the yellow pages.

The inspection takes at least an hour, and you should attend so the inspector can show and explain problems to you. You will also pay $75 or more for a termite inspection. Your lender requires it. Assuming that any issues found in the inspection were resolved, it is time to talk with your lender again.

Talk to the Lender—Again.

It is time to tell the lender that you have selected a house and negotiate your final terms. Get an agreement with your lender on:

- 15-year versus 30-year mortgage. If you take 30-year, make sure the lender allows you to pay it off in 15 years without penalty.

- FRM versus ARM. Take FRM if the interest rate is less than ten percent.

- Closing costs rolled into the mortgage, if that is what you want to do.

At this point, the lender may hire an appraiser.

DEFINITION: An appraiser is a real estate professional who specializes in providing opinions on value.

Your lender has an appraiser inspect the home and prepare an appraisal, estimating the value of the house. The appraiser bases the findings on the sale prices of similar houses in the same area and the potential rental income if the house is a duplex. You can often have the cost of the appraisal added to the closing costs, but your lender might require that you pay for it upfront. The lender may also have the property surveyed, costing about $350. This fee can be incorporated into your closing costs rather than paying it up front. The surveyor prepares an official diagram indicating property lines, sidewalks, and public utilities on the property. You will get a copy of the survey with all the papers you receive at the closing.

You need to select an insurance agent to handle your homeowner's insurance. Give the agent's contact information to the title company. Your lender will take care of paying your annual insurance bill for you by adding a small amount to your monthly mortgage payment. You will make an initial payment for insurance at closing as part of your closing costs. If you prefer, you can pay your insurance bill yourself, annually. Just let your lender know that is what you prefer. The lender may not wish to change the arrangement later.

CASE STUDY: LUKE V. ERICKSON

People ask me if I think that buying a home is a good investment. My answer is no. A home is your shelter and should be treated as such. I have no problem with someone making money when they sell their home, but I do have a problem with people selling their homes to make money. Due to opening and closing costs, the frequent buying and selling of homes

is unsustainable in the long run. You may say, "Well, over the last five years people have been doing that and have come out ahead."

I say, good for them. But what about all the other years before that? The real estate market would not have sustained such buying and selling. And what about five years from today? Nobody knows.

I realize that the real estate market throughout history has had a pretty consistent increase in value, but it cannot continue to escalate the way it has the past five or so years. Far too many people have been told that a home is a good investment, and they go into a home loan transaction with that attitude, especially subprime customers who have to pay a higher rate just to get a loan. In the end they will pay tens or hundreds of thousands of dollars more for their home than a prime borrower. For them, that home is not an investment. It is a poverty trap, sucking money out of their pockets every month for 30 years.

I have dealt with too many scams where individuals have lost their homes and been financially drained due to predatory home loans. Vulnerable individuals are duped into securing a mortgage loan with outrageous rates and fees. In the end they have been robbed of their financial security and their shelter.

Buy a home that you can afford and that you would not mind living in for a very long time. Anything else is too speculative. Do not gamble one of your primary needs on the bet that the market will rise to unusual heights. If homes are not such a good investment, what is safe or risk free? The truth is that any one investment can be risky.

CASE STUDY: LUKE V. ERICKSON

Even though it is safe from market volatility, a savings account is still subject to inflation risk because inflation decreases its value due. Aggressive stock investing is also risky, but it is due to market volatility.

There is a relatively safe middle ground including some CDs that can earn up to 5 percent, and some government bonds and notes. The safest investment is going to be a diversified portfolio of many different kinds of investments.

The time value of money (TVM) is so powerful that everyone who earns money should be saving for retirement. No amount is too small considering the compounding power that time will have on it. Even those over 65 could have several decades to use the TVM principle to their benefit.

Credit in some forms is not a convenience; it is a necessity. Most people simply cannot afford a home without a loan. Therefore, having credit in order to get the loan is important.

There is only one way to build credit consistently in my opinion—by paying the accounts off as quickly and frequently as possible. You do not need to go looking for credit accounts to open or to "get the right types of accounts." They will simply come to you as you go through life responsibly.

I do not believe that everyone needs a financial advisor. However, if they do not have the education or the patience and discipline to teach themselves personal finance principles, I would suggest a fee-only planner, someone who does not make commissions off products. But remember, a financial planner will not keep you from getting into trouble. Unless your planner is meeting with you frequently, chances are you can still make some pretty big mistakes and have no idea you are doing it.

Vulnerable individuals are duped into securing a mortgage loan with outrageous rates and fees. In the end, they have been robbed of their financial security and their shelter.

CASE STUDY: LUKE V. ERICKSON

Luke V. Erickson, Extension Educator

University of Idaho, Madison County

P.O. Box 580, Rexburg, ID 83440

208-359-6215

http://extension.ag.uidaho.edu/district4/madison.htm

University of Idaho
Extension

The Closing

DEFINITION:	Closing is the signing of papers and the transfer of money between buyer and seller.

You will need to bring a bank check for the down payment. If your closing costs were not rolled into your loan, you will also need to bring a bank check for the closing costs. For the mortgage money itself, ask your lender to wire the money directly to the title company. Although your home is considered an investment, you will eventually want to build up a true investment portfolio. Chapter Twelve will explain the basics.

NOW YOU KNOW
1. The banks will suggest that you can afford a home that is three times your annual income. A financial advisor may suggest a home worth 2.5 times your annual income.
2. If you cannot buy a home now, make home-owning a serious goal. Within two years, you can overcome most or all the obstacles.
3. Your lender can give an accurate estimate of closing costs on the purchase of the house you selected. This is called a "Good Faith Estimate." If they do not give it to you, ask for it.

4. Shop for a loan like you would shop for anything else by considering the cost and by comparing what you get. The cost is the interest rate you will be paying on the note, plus any fees the bank charges. Interest rates and fees vary from lender to lender.

5. Different banks charge different amounts of origination points, and some banks do not charge them at all.

6. Often there is no downside to using a realtor because the seller, not you, pays the fees.

7. You need a professional opinion of value to make sure you do not pay too much for the house.

8. Making an offer does not obligate you to buy the house, especially if the inspection turns up physical problems with it.

9. If the seller accepts your offer and signs the contract, you can proceed with having the house inspected and appraised. If the seller does not agree, you will receive a counteroffer. If you do not understand the offer, ask your real estate agent.

10. After you sign the contract, make sure to have the inspection, survey, and appraisal performed quickly, or you can lose your earnest money.

11. The earnest money is applied toward the purchase price if the deal goes through. If the deal does not go through, you can get your earnest money back, though this depends on how the contract is worded.

CHAPTER 12:
Investment Basics

Before building your portfolio, understand why you want to invest. Investing builds wealth. A $2,000 investment over 30 years at 11 percent interest will be worth more than $50,000. In 40 years it will be worth nearly $160,000. The same money hidden in a jar in the freezer will still be $2,000.

Next, you need to understand the tax implications of investing. Juan Ciscomani of Take Charge America Institute for Consumer Financial Education and Research, explains the current (2007) laws:

- Currently, capital gains on investments are 15 percent. If your marginal tax rate, i.e., the highest tax rate that you pay on your income to the federal and state government is higher than 15 percent, it makes sense to lean toward investments that yield capital gains.

- Corporate dividends are often taxed as ordinary income,

but right now, they are taxed at 15 percent making them a good value if your income is taxed at a rate higher than 15 percent.

- Mutual Funds "churn," that is, buying and selling are based on the portfolio rather than on the investor's tax situation. Therefore, you would be taxed based on your share of the mutual fund at your marginal tax rate.

- All retirement options such as IRAs and 401(k)s are funded with before tax dollars but are taxed on retirement. Traditionally, income is lower at retirement, reducing the tax percentage one would pay. For a Roth IRA or Roth 401(k), after-tax money funds these two retirement account options, but the appreciation in these accounts is never taxed.

Investing based on taxes is not the way to go—the best way to invest is to find a sound investment.

The problem is finding that sound investment and then figuring out how to go about investing in it. Have you ever looked in the bookstore for books on investing? The amount of information out there is overwhelming and often frightening to those who have never ventured into investing before. There are some general rules that will help you simplify the process.

Make Investing a Habit

Your investments can be part of your savings plan. The way to succeed at investing is to put money into your investment accounts regularly. Think about the money you save in a way that creates a desire to invest. Two movies a month is $720 a year and $720 in savings over 30 years at 8 percent is almost $8000. Lose the car payment of $200 a month ($2,400 per year) that $2,400 savings over 30 years at 8 percent is just over $26,000.

For many investments, you can count on an 11 percent return on average. That means your $720 would be $19,000 in 30 years and your $2,400 would be $64,000. If thinking like that does not get you excited about investing, maybe investing is not for you.

How Long Does It Take? The Rule of 72

To determine how long it takes for your money to grow, you will need to know the percentage that your money will earn. Here are some average rates of return (over the last 100 years) for some of the more traditional investments:

- U.S. Treasury Bills – 3.8 percent

- Money Market Funds – 3.8 percent

- Long-Term Government Bonds – 5 percent

- Stocks – 11 percent

- Well-diversified Mutual Funds – 12 percent

After you know the rate of return, you can determine how long it will take your money to grow using the Rule of 72.

DEFINITION:	The rule of 72 is a quick way to determine how long it takes for an investment to double in value with a given yield.

Divide 72 by the percent earned and you will know how many years it takes to double initial principal.

For example, $10,000 earning 8 percent will double in 9 years.

72 divided by 8 equals 9 years.

$10,000 earning 12 percent will double in 6 years.

72 divided by 12 equals 6 years.

An average rate of return of 11 percent—the average rate of return for stocks—can triple your money in 10 years. Using the Rule of 72, investing $10,000 at 11 percent will take 6.5 years to double but only 3.5 to triple. This is due to the power of compounding interest.

Investing $1 in a U.S. government bond at 5 percent for 50 years will return $12. That same $1 put into a stock averaging 11 percent will be worth $238 due to compounding interest.

Investing $1,000 in a:

- 5 percent bond for 50 years returns $12,000
- 11 percent stock for 50 years returns $238,000

Now, that is a difference.

Long-term Investments

DEFINITION: Short-term investments are accounts that are liquid; you can get your money in cash in your hands easily.

Short-term investments are savings accounts, CDs, and MMAs. The easier you can get your money, the lower the interest rate. Short-term investments are good for short-term goals such as:

- An emergency fund

- Down payment on a house

- College tuition

- A family vacation

- Another car (used)

DEFINITION:	Long-term investments are for long-term goals like retirement. The two major vehicles for long-term investing are stocks and bonds.

Bonds are fixed; the rate of return is set at time of purchase. Stocks fluctuate; rate of return changes daily even hourly. There are different ways to invest in stocks:

- Individual Stocks

- Mutual Funds

- Index Funds

With individual stocks, your money is the only money going toward any particular stock. If you buy ten shares of IBM, then you own ten shares of IBM. With mutual funds, your money is pooled with other clients' money. When your mutual fund buys stock, you are a partial owner of each stock. There are many types of mutual funds: some are conservative; some are more volatile; some are strictly U.S. stocks; and some have foreign stocks.

Research before choosing a mutual fund; find a fund that invests in the types of stocks you prefer and check for any fees.

Index is similar to mutual funds, but the investments are made based on a particular index such as the Dow Jones, the S&P, or the NASDAQ.

DEFINITION:	Indexes are a group of stocks that represent the current U.S. economy.

The Dow Jones' components are 30 companies. the S&P, 500; NASDAQ, 3,200.

Three Rules for Investing

Diversify. Reduce risk by spreading money among many investments, such as stocks, bonds, and short-term investments. Diversified portfolios tend to be less risky over the long-term.

You will also want to diversify in each type of asset class. Buy different types of bonds and stocks. By diversifying within an asset class, you decrease your risk and any particular investment has less chance to affect the performance of your portfolio.

The less volatile the portfolio, the higher the compound return. Even if two portfolios have the same average rate of return, the less volatile of the two will produce a higher rate of return.

If you have a portfolio that averages ten percent, but does so by having one year at twenty percent, the next at zero percent and the next at ten percent, you will have less money than if you had a portfolio that consistently had a ten percent return for three years. It is difficult to find an investment at ten percent that is so steady, but the closer your investments get to an even rate, the better.

To reduce major swings in your portfolio, choose investments that do not move together. For example, when large company stocks go up, government bonds tend to go down, and visa versa. Having investments in your portfolio that move in this way helps to keep your rate of return steady.

Global diversification reduces risk. Throughout the history of the stock market, there have been periods of time that the U.S. equity market has outperformed foreign markets and vice versa.

Diversifying globally allows you to reduce the risk of losing in one country's market.

Investment Sources

As you are working to create an efficient portfolio, there are several sources that can help you evaluate investments.

1. Morningstar provides data on more than 15,000 mutual funds, 8,000 stocks, and 20,000 variable annuity/life sub-accounts worldwide. Products include print publications, software, and Internet solutions. **www.morningstar.com**

2. Value Line publishes more than a dozen print and electronic products on investment research on stocks, mutual funds, options and convertibles, and offers a family of no-load mutual funds. The company is best known for The Value Line Investment Survey. **www.valueline.com**

3. Investor's Business Daily (IBD) is an investment newspaper known for its innovative stock tables. Investor's Business Daily provides information previously available only to pension and mutual funds, banks, insurance companies and government organizations. **www.investors.com**

Now that you have the basics of investing, Chapter Thirteen will explain in more detail stocks, bonds, mutual funds, and other investments.

CASE STUDY: JUAN CISCOMANI

The biggest mistake in investing is not being able to properly identify when to invest. I met two university students who would use their grocery and rent money to buy and sell stocks online. Getting into the stock market at a young age is not a bad idea; however, these two students were not being smart in risking their only capital to go into the stock

exchange arena.

They were not able to clearly identify the right time in their lives to begin investing. They became deep in credit card debt, which provoked them to keep investing in order to pay their debt. They were viewing investing as gambling.

Some people expect their investment to have an immediate growth. Sometimes it happens, but when it does not, they lose patience and pull out before their money has had time to grow.

Here are some more common mistakes:

- Getting into the stock market without knowing what you want to get out of it or without setting investing goals.

- Lack of due diligence. When people buy a car, they spend time researching, test-driving, and asking friends, but the same discipline is not applied to mutual funds, stocks, or real estate.

- Not understanding your risk tolerance. Determine what you want and what your risk tolerance is, and invest accordingly. Are you willing to lose half your portfolio for a 50 percent chance at 300 percent gains? Do you want guaranteed 5 percent returns?

Every investment has some sort of risk; clearly there are some with a higher risk factor than others. Different investments can be affected by market conditions like recession, inflation, global events, and interest rates. CDs and bonds tend to be lower risk and

CASE STUDY: JUAN CISCOMANI

offer a lower return rate. Stocks are the most risky investment. Any of these investments is valid as long as you have a plan, do your research, and understand your risk tolerance.

Mistakes are not just made in investing. There are many common mistakes that young adults make with their finances. Credit cards are erroneously viewed as income. It is much easier to swipe a credit card than to pay cash. Doing so leads into debt. Do not get me wrong—credit is important. Using credit cards, on the other hand, is not.

The financing terms of a home or car purchase are directly tied to an individual's credit. Good credit leads to low interest rates. Bad credit leads to high interest rates and higher monthly payments. Credit influences an employer's decision to hire or not hire an individual. Some graduate programs check for credit. In today's society, it is vital to establish credit.

The best way to establish credit is to open a credit card with your bank. Use the credit card to pay for groceries, gas, and the cell phone bill, paying off the balance at the end of the month. Low debt, consistent usage, timely payments, and manageable open lines of credit help you have good credit.

One key step to avoid debt is creating a weekly or monthly budget. Identifying needs versus wants is a key element. Recognizing your needs and wants can enable you to allocate your funds properly and make wiser spending decisions. Understand the different ways of getting into debt.

I met a college student who did not want student loans. He told me, "I did not want to owe any money to the federal government, especially with the high interest rates (during this time Stafford student loans averaged between four percent and five percent), so I just used my credit card." After talking to him for a while, I discovered that the APR on his credit card was 18.99 percent. He made a foolish decision. Even though some debt was inevitable, there was a much better way to pay for his school expenses.

CASE STUDY: JUAN CISCOMANI

After getting into debt trouble, there is no universal strategy to fix your credit rating. It all depends on what got you there. If your credit is bad because of having too many credit cards and they are at their limits, start paying them off and closing them out.. If bad credit status is due to late payments, start paying on time. If too many credit inquiries are causing bad credit, let your credit rest. Fixing credit it is not a one-week or a one-month process. Improving credit takes time, patience, and faithful determination. You must create a plan to improve your credit and not deviate from the plan. Have a financial advisor look at your finances so that you can have a clear understanding of your financial situation, enabling you to make intelligent decisions.

Even though it is safe from market volatility, a savings account is still subject to inflation risk because inflation decreases its value due. Aggressive stock investing is also risky, but it is due to market volatility.

There is a relatively safe middle ground including some CDs that can earn up to five percent, and some government bonds and notes. The safest investment is going to be a diversified portfolio of many different kinds of investments.

The time value of money (TVM) is so powerful that everyone who earns money should be saving for retirement. No amount is too small considering the compounding power that time will have on it. Even those over 65 could have several decades to use the TVM principle to their benefit.

Credit in some forms is not a convenience; it is a necessity. Most people simply cannot afford a home without a loan. Therefore, having credit in order to get the loan is important.

There is only one way to build credit consistently in my opinion—by paying the accounts off as quickly and frequently as possible. You do not need to go looking for credit accounts to open or to "get the right types of accounts." They will simply come to you as you go through life responsibly.

CASE STUDY: JUAN CISCOMANI

I do not believe that everyone needs a financial advisor. However, if they do not have the education or the patience and discipline to teach themselves personal finance principles, I would suggest a fee-only planner, someone who does not make commissions off products. But remember, a financial planner will not keep you from getting into trouble. Unless your planner is meeting with you frequently, chances are you can still make some pretty big mistakes and have no idea you are doing it.

Juan Ciscomani

Senior Instructional Specialist

Credit-Wise Cats

Take Charge America Institute for Consumer Financial Education and Research

John and Doris Norton School of Family and Consumer Sciences

The University of Arizona

Phone: 520-626-5376

Fax: 520-626-3209

http://tcainstitute.org/

NOW YOU KNOW

1. Your investments are part of your savings plan. To succeed at investing, put money into your investment accounts regularly.

2. To determine money growth, you need to know the percentage your money earns.

3. When you purchase individual stocks, you make the decisions as to what to buy and why, or you have a broker do it.

4. Mutual funds are companies that receive your money and determine where to invest it for you.

5. Diversified portfolios are low-risk over the long-term.

6. To reduce the major swings of your portfolio, you need to choose investments that do not move together.

CHAPTER 13:
Building Your Portfolio

How to Pick Your Stocks

Blue Chip stocks are well known.

DEFINITION:	Blue chip stocks get their name from poker. Blue chips are the most valuable. Blue chip stocks are issued by a well established firms.

They can provide verifiable records of payments on dividends. A check of Moody's dividend record shows that many have paid in excess of ten percent year in and year out despite changes in the economy.

When choosing your stocks, you need to look for total return, i.e., performance in terms of long-term capital gains and dividend growth. Your total return should equal inflation plus seven percent.

There Are Three Ways to Purchase Stock:

1. Go to a financial planner.

2. Buy them on the Internet.

3. Buy them directly from the company.

The key to buying stocks is discipline, both in buying and selling. You must make these decisions without emotion.

Understanding Bonds

DEFINITION: A bond is a debt security, similar to an IOU.

A bond is like a mortgage except you are the lender instead of the borrower. When you purchase a bond, you are lending money to a government, municipality, corporation, federal agency, or other entity known as the issuer. You then become a creditor of the company, as a stockholder would be. In return for the loan, the issuer promises to pay you a specified rate of interest, known as the coupon, during the life of the bond and to repay the face value of the bond when it comes due. The coupon is the price they pay you to use your money.

Bonds may be secured or unsecured. A secured bond is backed by collateral, ensuring that capital will be available to pay the principal on the bond. Corporate bonds and municipal bonds may be secured or unsecured. Federal government bonds are unsecured. Unsecured bonds are not backed by collateral, but pay higher yields. Some companies do not have enough assets to collateralize. Other companies are established and are trusted to repay their debts. As for governments, they can raise taxes if they need to pay off bondholders. The federal government can print more money to meet its needs.

All debt securities are issued with a fixed face amount; however, the issuer often sells them at a discount, giving the investor extra incentive to purchase the issue. For example, a debt can be given a value of $500 but be sold for only $450.

Terminology You Should Know

Short-term. In bond maturities, one to five years.

Intermediate-term. In bond maturities, five to ten years.

Long-term. In bond maturities, more than ten years.

Par. The value of a bond assigned by the issuer; also called face value.

Original issue discount. A bond with an offering price that is below par value.

Coupon. A bond's interest rate.

Yield to maturity. The fully compounded annual rate of return paid out over a bond's life, from purchase date to maturity, including appreciation, depreciation, and earnings. It is the most comprehensive measure of yield.

Floating-interest rate. A variable interest rate.

Floating-interest bond. A bond with an interest rate that changes each quarter to reflect economic conditions.

Fixed-interest bond. A bond with an interest rate that stays the same over its life span.

Corporate bond. A bond issued by a corporation and backed by the company's credit and assets. These can include:

- **Industrial bond.** A bond issued to finance construction for manufacturing or commercial activity.

- **Collateral trust bond.** A corporate bond backed by financial assets (such as a securities portfolio) of a corporation. These assets are by a third-party trustee.

- **Equipment trust certificate.** A corporate bond secured by company equipment. Among the most common issuers are airlines and railroads that need to finance new purchases of equipment. The equipment bought may be used as collateral.

- **Mortgage bond.** A secured corporate bond that is backed by real estate. Because mortgage bond collateral provides a clear claim on a company's assets, these bonds are considered secure and high-grade.

- **Junk bond.** Refers to the quality of a bond that is a speculative, high yielding, and issued by a company that often finances its growth and operations with debt. Ratings companies often assign low grades to these bonds.

Municipal bonds. They are issued by a state or local government or its subdivisions. Municipal bonds are issued to raise money for industrial projects, housing, residential construction, and general revenue. The interest earned on a municipal bond is often free of federal income tax, and possibly of local and state taxes. These can include:

- **Revenue bond.** A bond sold by a municipality to finance projects; bridges, hospitals, power plants, and other local services. Also called limited obligation bonds, revenue bonds are secured by the revenue generated by those projects.

- **General obligation bond (GO bond).** An unsecured municipal bond. The payment of interest and principal are guaranteed by the taxing authority and credit worthiness of the issuer. GO bonds finance municipal operations.

- **Industrial-development bond.** A municipal bond sold to raise money for facilities for private enterprises. These bonds attract industries to areas that need economic development.

- **MBIA-insured bonds, AMBAC-insured bonds.** Municipal bonds guaranteed by either the Municipal Bond Insurance Association or the American Municipal Bond Assurance Corporation, two major bond insurance companies. To receive insurance from either of these groups, the municipality must take out a policy and pay a premium.

Government bond. A bond sold by the U.S. Government. They are rated the highest of all bonds. They are used to finance federal projects. They include:

- **Treasury bond (T-bond).** A bond issued by the U.S. Treasury to meet the government's financial needs. T- bonds are considered the safest bonds and are very popular with investors. They have maturities lasting from 10 to 30 years.

- **Treasury note (T-note).** An intermediate-term federal government debt, similar to a T-bond but maturing in one to ten years.

- **Agency bond.** A bond issued by an agency of the federal government, such as the Student Loan Marketing Association (Sallie Mae). Government agencies are corporations, and the government does not guarantee agency bonds.

Bond Maturity

Unlike stocks, bonds have finite lifetimes. The issuers of bonds determine the lifetimes before they sell the bonds to investors.

DEFINITION: The date on which a bond comes due is called maturity. Some people use the word "maturity" to refer to the lifetime itself. For example, they may say that a particular bond has a ten year maturity.

Maturities range from one month to as long as fifty years. Some different maturity times for different bonds are as follows:

- Corporate bonds—10 to 40 years

- Municipal bonds—1 to over 20 years

- Municipal notes—1 month to 1 year

- U.S. Government agency bonds—3 years and over

- U.S. Treasury bonds—10 to 30 years

- U.S. Treasury notes—2 to 10 years

Mutual Funds

In the '40s, Wall Street was allowed to create management companies now known as Mutual Funds.

DEFINITION: A mutual fund is a collection of stocks, bonds, or other securities owned by a group of investors and managed by a professional investment company.

Most experts agree that as an individual investor, you would need from $50,000 to $100,000 to create a suitably diversified portfolio. Mutual funds can offer big investment opportunities for small amounts of money—as little as $25 a month.

Why Invest in Mutual Funds?

Mutual funds offer opportunities to help achieve financial goals through:

1. **Diversification:** A mutual fund may hold stocks in 50 or more companies and in many different industries. One of the fund's stocks' doing poorly should not affect the entire fund. For the individual investor, the amount of disposable income and investment knowledge required to accomplish similar diversification would be mind-boggling. Also, sharing expenses with like-minded investors, through a mutual fund, significantly reduces your investment cost. Because a mutual fund combines the assets it holds in trust for you and other investors, it is known as an "institutional trader" and as such can buy securities at wholesale prices; bulk shopping, investment style.

2. **Professional Management:** Mutual funds are run by a team of professionals or an individual manager or who brings relevant academic qualifications and years of experience in analyzing data to choose securities to meet the fund's objectives and to decide when to trade the holdings, both daunting tasks to attempt on your own. By investing in a well-managed mutual fund, you share the expense of hiring a manager with a proven track record.

3. **Performance:** The attraction of mutual funds is higher returns on investment dollar, especially during periods of low interest rates. Do not assume all mutual funds provide higher returns. Many do; some do not.

4. **Ease of Investment:** Buying a mutual fund is not complicated and can be done in person, by telephone, or by mail. Most mutual fund groups offer toll-free telephone assistance. You may prefer speaking with someone in person and having them complete the necessary paperwork.

5. **Liquidity.** It is easy to get at your money. Units can be redeemed at any time, and your money will be available within five business days. Real-estate funds may take

longer. After the mutual fund company receives the authorization, your money will be sent to you in check form or deposited directly into your bank account. Some companies allow redemption by telephone or fax, if you provided authorization at time of purchase.

6. **Flexible Investing:** The minimum initial investment for a mutual fund ranges from $25 to $500, with $500 being the norm. Subsequent investments start at $25. The amount and the frequency depend on the options offered by the company.

7. **Record Keeping:** All mutual fund companies provide unit holders with regular statements detailing all transactions, income earned, and the total value of all funds held. When you buy or sell units in a mutual fund, you automatically receive written confirmation. Unit holders also receive yearly statements detailing the tax status of all earnings from the fund, including dividends and capital gains information.

So, What is It Going to Cost?

Before you buy units in any mutual fund, know exactly how much it is going to cost. All charges are listed in the simplified prospectus. All mutual funds charge a management fee, a percentage of the fund's total assets that pays the administrative costs, wages, and bonuses of fund managers. Funds charge 0.5 percent for some money-market funds to nearly 4 percent for certain international funds. Management fees are deducted before the quoted performance numbers are calculated.

Assume you bought units in a fund with total assets of $2 billion and a management fee of 2 percent. The management fee for that particular fund would be $40 million annually. Management fees are non-negotiable.

DEFINITION: A load is nothing more than a sales charge.

Management fees for load funds may vary according to which option you choose. There are three types of loads:

1. A front-end load is a sales charge that you pay at the time of purchase. This sales commission can be as high as nine percent, although most companies recommend a maximum of five percent to six percent. The amount is negotiable with your mutual fund representative. When you see the words "maximum" or "up to" next to fees, it means you can bargain. This sales charge is deducted from the amount you invest. If you have $5,000 to invest and pay a front-end load of 3 percent, the actual amount of money invested is $4,850 ($5000 minus $150).

2. A back-end load is the fee charged to investors when they redeem their units. This fee is often staggered, with earlier redemptions paying a higher fee, a policy designed to discourage early withdrawals. A typical range starts at five percent or six percent for redemptions during the first two years and decreases to zero percent after seven to ten years. The redemption fee schedule given below is typical of many funds.

1st year	6.0 percent
2nd year	5.5 percent
3rd year	5.0 percent
4th year	4.5 percent
5th year	4.0 percent
6th year	3.0 percent
7th year	2.0 percent
Thereafter	Nil

If you opt for the back-end load, your entire $5,000 goes to work for you immediately.

3. **No-Load Option** is a no-sales-commission option. Again,

check the Management Expense Ratio (MER). It will probably be higher than either the front-end or back-end load MERs. Over the longer term, this could significantly decrease your returns.

DEFINITION:	A trailer fee is the annual service commission paid by the mutual fund company to your sales representative.

This fee is paid as long as you hold units in the fund. These fees often range between 0.25 and 1 percent and are paid out of the fund's management expenses. A trailer fee is a service commission. To earn these fees, your salesperson should be providing you with ongoing services such as answering questions about your account, tax information, the performance of your funds, and other related matters.

If there is anything you do not fully understand about a fund's fees, call or visit your fund company's nearest office to get an idea of the type of service and attitude of the company. If you are not satisfied with the answers you receive or with the level of service, you may want to reconsider buying that particular fund. If you are buying from an independent sales representative, you also need to know if he or she is being paid a trailer fee. If so, make sure you receive ongoing service.

Types of Funds

Money market and Treasury bill funds are the most conservative mutual funds. They invest primarily in government (or equally safe) securities. These funds often pay two or three percentage points higher rates of return than savings accounts and are extremely safe.

Fixed income funds invest in some combination of Treasury bills, debentures, bonds, and mortgages. The aim of fixed income funds is to provide high, regular income payments with the possibility of capital gains.

Equity funds invest in common and preferred shares of companies and are recommended for investors seeking long-term growth through capital gains. An investment time of at least five years is often recommended for this type of fund.

Balanced funds provide a combination of income and growth by investing in a mixed portfolio of common stock, preferred shares, bonds, and cash. This fund is suitable for investors with limited dollars wanting a more diversified portfolio in one fund.

Dividend funds invest in dividend-paying preferred shares of corporations and in common shares that are expected to yield a high level of dividend income. These funds have potential for long-term capital growth. Dividend funds also receive preferential tax treatment.

Global and international funds invest in money-market securities and in bond and stock markets in various countries and regions of the world. These funds offer investors the opportunity to increase returns through extra diversification.

Choosing Your Fund

Before you invest in any fund, there are two important factors to consider: the fund's investment objectives and its level of risk. Both should be given equal weight when making an investment decision. Every mutual fund has a specific investment objective — safety of capital, income, or growth. The fund manager buys and sells securities to attain that goal. The three fund objectives are:

1. Safety of capital funds — look for ways to protect your initial investment from loss.

2. Income funds — provide investors with stable and regular monthly or quarterly payments.

3. Growth funds — invest in equity securities to increase the

value of the fund's assets and provide investors with long-term capital gains.

Some funds seek to provide a combination of all three objectives, in one package.

Decide which investment objectives match your own and concentrate on those particular funds.

Mutual funds never invest at random, and neither should you. The clearer you define your investment objectives, the easier it will be to identify appropriate mutual funds. To find the funds that are best for you, you have to understand the concept of investment risk.

DEFINITION: Risk is the possibility that an investment may go down in value or not perform as well as expected.

No investment is risk free. Even money lying securely in a savings account is at risk from inflation. Some common risk factors are:

- **Credit risk.** The possibility that the company holding your money will not pay the interest or dividend due or the principal amount when it matures.

- **Inflation risk.** The risk that the dollar you get when you sell will buy less than the dollar you originally invested.

- **Interest-rate risk.** The possibility that a fixed debt instrument, such as a bond, will decline in value because of a rise in interest rates.

- **Market risk.** The risk that the unit price or value of your investment will decrease.

One fundamental rule applies to all investments. The smaller the risk, the smaller your potential returns; the higher the risk, the higher the potential reward. The further away from your financial goals, the more risk you can afford to take because the ups and downs of financial markets tend to even out over time. Historically the stock market has risen steadily regardless of its temporary declines. The closer to your financial goals the less time you will have to make up any losses.

In addition to investment objectives and risk, there is volatility.

DEFINITION:	Volatility is a measure of the historical variability in a fund's rate of return compared with similar funds. When you take into account the returns on all mutual funds, some funds will have wider swings in returns than others.

Factors that can contribute to a fund's volatility include the type of assets held, degree of diversification, sector, country or region of investment, use of derivatives, turnover and quality of portfolio holdings, and management investment style. A fund that invests in U.S. Government treasury bills is less volatile than one that invests in shares of small new companies. A fund that invests in many countries is going to be less volatile than a fund that invests in one country.

Your goal should be to invest in a fund with a good track record (over the past 20 to 40 years) that meets your investment objectives and has a level of volatility that you can live with comfortably. Two funds can average the same return but perform very differently. One fund may earn 11 percent one year and 13 percent the second. The other fund may earn 25.4 percent the first year but have a return of 0 percent the second. Through the law of compounding, both funds average 12 percent a year. Most investors prefer the steady performer.

Initial Public Offerings

DEFINITION:	An initial public offering (IPO) is the first sale of a corporation's stock to outside investors.

Offering an IPO does not necessarily mean that a company is a new business. It means that the company is offering shares of ownership to investors outside the corporate family for the first time.

Buying shares the first time they are offered to the public has considerable natural appeal, especially in a bull market, tempting investors with potential phenomenal short-term returns and exposure to exciting new companies and industries. And since the early 1980s, privatizations of state-owned corporations around the world have become an additional source of new issues, providing investors with the opportunity to get low-priced stakes in big, stable businesses, often the dominant incumbents in core sectors of the global economy; however, is investing in an IPO right for you?

Most businesses are privately owned. They do not have outside investors. A few people, who may be management or employees and members of their respective families, own all the outstanding stock. Such corporations are called closely held corporations. These companies are often small, but some are nationally recognized names such as AVIS Rent-a-Car and United Parcel Service.

When a privately held corporation needs additional capital, it can borrow cash or sell stock to raise needed funds. Often going public is the best choice for a growing business. Compared to the costs of borrowing large sums of money for ten years or more, the costs of an initial public offering are small. The capital raised never has to be repaid. When a company sells its stock publicly, there is also the possibility for appreciation of the share price due to market factors not directly related to the company.

What to Look for When Choosing an IPO

As with any investment, you must do your homework carefully. Remember that an initial public offering is a cheap way to raise capital. Investing in an IPO is not always best for the investor. Before signing that check, be clear about your purpose for the investment. Are you investing for income, long-term growth, or short-term capital gains? The offering's financials will tell the story.

- As an income investor, you need to examine the company's potential for profits and its dividend policy. You are looking for steadily rising profits that will be distributed to shareholders regularly.

- A growth investor evaluates the company's growth plan, earnings, and potential for retained earnings. You are looking for potential steady increase in profits that are reinvested for further expansion.

- A speculator looks for short-term capital gains. You look for potential of an early market breakthrough or discovery that will send the price up quickly with little care about a rapid decline. You are not going to be in it that long. Companies that have fad products often fit the bill.

Risks of an IPO

Before investing in an initial public offering, you need to ask yourself some questions.

1. How much do you actually know about this company? A Wall Street sage once said, "Never invest money in anything you do not understand." You may understand all about how an IPO works, but what do you actually know about the business of the company in which you plan to invest? Before it went public, the only shareholders in a privately held company were the management, employees and their families. They all know about the business; they are in it. Before investing, you need to learn the fundamentals of the business.

2. What is their product or service? Who are their competitors?

3. What is their share of the market for their product?

4. What is the likelihood they will succeed with their newfound capital?

There Are Three Kinds of Risk Related to the Company

1. **Business Risk:** Does this company have a sound business plan and management with education, training, and experience sufficient to execute the plan?

2. **Financial Risk:** Is this company solvent with sufficient capital to weather short-term business setbacks?

3. **Market Risk:** Are other investors likely to buy this stock on the secondary market? Does this company possess sufficient appeal to investors in the current market environment (income, growth, or short-term capital gains)? How long is the attraction likely to last?

What Information Should You Get Before Investing?

The more information you have, the better decision you will be able to make. Keep in mind that the original stockholders are insiders. Among the information you want to know:

- **Business Operations:** What is management like? Do the employees like to work there? Is there a large turnover in the labor force? How do customers perceive the company? How do Dunn and Bradstreet and the Better Business Bureau rate the company?

- **Financial Operations:** What is the company's credit history? Are they in default on any debts? Have the owners invested sufficient capital to give them a financial stake in the company's success? How does this company's expenses compare to their competition?

- **Marketability:** Would you buy and use their product? Who would? Is their product a long-term commodity or just a fad? Can you buy the IPO shares directly from the issuer?

A substantial advantage can be gained if you can purchase IPO shares directly from an issuer. This could save you mark-up and commissions used to pay for marketing the offering. By taking the time to answer each of the previous questions, you gain valuable information that will help you decide whether this IPO is a suitable investment for you.

Where Can I Find Information About The Company?

Federal law states that all initial public offerings are required to be accompanied or preceded by a prospectus.

DEFINITION:	The prospectus is the official offering document that contains all material information about the company and its offering.

If you are looking for an IPO as an investment, you should be familiar with the following:

- IPOs are introduced in the financial press with a tombstone advertisement. This contains the bare bones information, including the name of the stock, the issuer, and how to obtain a prospectus.

- Information about the offering is available on the Securities and Exchange Commission's Edgar database.

- Many companies have their own Web sites that provide information to their customers and prospective investors.

- Barron's, The Wall Street Journal, Investor's Daily, and other financial periodicals report on companies going public.

Precious Metals and Commodities

Historically, precious metals and commodities have not been a good way to make money.

> **DEFINITION:** Commodities are things like bales of hay, or cotton, sugar, gold, or different metals.

I recommend that as a beginning investor you avoid commodities and precious metals and concentrate on investing in money market accounts, savings accounts, and then into some form of stocks or bonds whether it is mutual funds or direct. You need to have traditional investments before getting into real estate, commodities, or precious metals.

Investing is not easy. This chapter just touched on some of the basics. It is important for you to educate yourself in investing or hire a financial consultant in order to invest your money wisely. If you do decide to go it alone, you want to watch out for the investment scams listed in the next chapter.

NOW YOU KNOW
1. When choosing stocks, you need to look for total return, i.e., performance in terms of long-term capital gains and dividend growth. Your total return should equal inflation plus seven percent.
2. When you purchase a bond, you are lending money to a government, municipality, corporation, federal agency, or other entity known as the issuer.
3. Unlike stocks, bonds have finite lifetimes. The issuers of bonds determine the lifetimes before they sell the bonds to investors.
4. When you put money into a mutual fund, it is pooled with other investors' money. A mutual fund gives you greater purchasing power than investing on your own.
5. Invest in a fund with a good track record (over the past 20 to 40 years) that meets your investment objectives and has a level of volatility that you can comfortably live with.
6. IPOs are not for every investor. They may provide an opportunity for substantial gain for the knowledgeable investor, but the unwary investor is likely to get burned.

CHAPTER 14:
Avoiding Investment Scams

Investment scams run rampant. Anyone can be a victim.

Juan Ciscomani of Take Charge America Institute for Consumer Financial Education and Research explains what he has seen concerning scams:

> An elderly couple, Joe and Ann, were taken in by a long-term care insurance scam. A salesman came to the door offering a one-year policy for $2,000. Joe agreed to the sale and wrote out a check. The problem was that there was no company. Luckily for them, it was just $2,000 and they could afford the loss.
>
> Joe and Ann should have talked with someone before handing the check over. The lesson to learn from this is to do your research. Know what you are buying and know that what you are buying is legitimate.

Unfortunately, there are a number of scams in today's financial society. A popular one is the Phishing scams. These prey on the one percent of people who do not read an e-mail thoroughly, and send personal bank account information in the hopes of a quick source of money.

By using all the salesman techniques of putting time pressure on the recipient and appealing to their greed, the perpetrators bring age-old guises into a new era.

Each year, con artists find new and inventive ways to rip people off. More harmful than feeling conned is the financial devastation it can cause. It is essential to be savvy enough to see through scams and wise enough to check out all financial opportunities with someone you trust.

In this chapter we will explore some of the more common investment scams identified by the FBI and some ideas to avoid them.

Telemarketing Fraud

When you send money to people you do not know or give personal or financial information to unknown callers, you increase your chances of becoming a victim of telemarketing fraud.

Warning signs—what a caller may tell you:

- "You must act now or the offer will not be good."

- "You have won a free gift, vacation, or prize." But you have to pay for "postage and handling" or other charges.

- "You must send money, give a credit card or bank account number, or have a check picked up by courier." You may hear this before you have had a chance to consider the offer carefully.

- "You do not need to check out the company with anyone." The callers say you do not need to speak to anyone including your family, lawyer, accountant, local Better Business Bureau, or consumer protection agency.

- "You do not need any written information about their company or their references."

- "You cannot afford to miss this high-profit, no-risk offer."

If you hear these or similar lines from a telephone salesperson, just say "no thank you," and hang up the phone.

It is very difficult to get your money back if you have been cheated over the phone. Before you buy anything by telephone, remember:

- Do not buy from an unknown company. Legitimate businesses understand that you want more information about their company and are happy to comply.

- Always ask for and wait until you receive written material about any offer or charity. If you get brochures about costly investments, ask someone whose financial advice you trust to review them.

- Always check out unknown companies with your local consumer protection agency, Better Business Bureau, state Attorney General, the National Fraud Information Center, or other watchdog groups. Unfortunately, not all bad businesses can be identified through these organizations.

- Obtain a salesperson's name, business identity, telephone number, street address, mailing address, and business license number before you transact business. Verify the accuracy of these items.

- Before you give money to a charity or make an investment, find out what percentage of the money is paid in commissions and what percentage goes to the charity or investment.

- Before you send money, ask yourself a simple question. "What guarantee do I actually have that this solicitor will use my money in the manner we agreed on?"

- You must not be asked to pay in advance for services. Pay for services only after they are delivered.

- Some con artists will send a messenger to your home to pick up money, claiming it is part of their service to you. In reality, they are taking your money without leaving any trace of who they are or where they can be reached.

- Always take your time making a decision. Legitimate companies will not pressure you to make a snap decision.

- Do not pay for a free prize. If a caller tells you the payment is for taxes, he or she is violating federal law.

- Before you receive your next sales pitch, decide what your limits are — the kinds of financial information you will and will not give out on the telephone.

- It is never rude to wait and think about an offer. Be sure to talk over big investments offered by telephone salespeople with a trusted friend, family member, or financial advisor.

- Never respond to an offer you do not understand thoroughly.

- Never send money or give out personal information such as credit card numbers and expiration dates, bank account numbers, dates of birth, or social security numbers to unfamiliar companies or unknown persons.

- Your personal information is often brokered to telemarketers through third parties.

- If you have information about a fraud, report it to state, local, or federal law enforcement agencies.

Nigerian Letter or "419" Fraud

A letter, mailed from Nigeria, offers the recipient the opportunity to share in a percentage of millions of dollars that the author, a self-proclaimed government official, is trying to transfer illegally out of Nigeria. You are encouraged to send information, such as blank letterhead stationery, bank name, and account numbers and other identifying information using a fax number provided in the letter. Some of these letters have also been received via e-mail. The scheme relies on convincing you to send money to Nigeria in several installments of increasing amounts for a variety of reasons. Payment of taxes, bribes to government officials, and legal fees are often described in great detail with the promise that all expenses will be reimbursed as soon as the funds are spirited out of Nigeria. The perpetrators have been known to use the personal information and checks received to impersonate the victim, draining bank accounts and credit card balances.

The schemes violate section 419 of the Nigerian criminal code, hence the label "419 Fraud." Some Tips to Avoid Nigerian Letter or "419 Fraud":

- If you receive a letter from Nigeria asking you to send personal or banking information, do not reply. Send the letter to the U.S. Secret Service or the FBI.

- If you know someone who is corresponding in one of these schemes, encourage that person to contact the FBI or the U.S. Secret Service as soon as possible.

- Be skeptical of individuals representing themselves as Nigerian or foreign government officials asking for your help in placing large sums of money in overseas bank accounts.

- Do not believe the promise of large sums of money for your cooperation.

- Guard your account information carefully.

Identity Fraud

Identity fraud occurs when someone assumes your identity to perform a criminal act. Criminals get your identity from a variety of sources, such as the theft of your wallet, your trash, or from credit or bank information. They may ask you for the information in person, by telephone, or on the Internet. You can minimize your risk of loss by following a few simple hints.

- Never throw away ATM receipts, credit statements, credit cards, or bank statements in a usable form.

- Never give your credit card number over the telephone unless you make the call.

- Reconcile your bank account monthly and notify your bank of discrepancies immediately.

- Keep a list of telephone numbers to call to report the loss or theft of your wallet, credit cards, and other personal information.

- Report unauthorized financial transactions to your bank, credit card company, and the police as soon as you detect them.

- Review a copy of your credit report at least once a year. Notify the credit bureau in writing of any questionable entries and follow through until they are explained or removed.

- If your identity has been assumed, ask the credit bureau to print a statement in your credit report.

- If you know of anyone who receives mail from credit card companies or banks in the names of others, report it to local or federal law enforcement.

Advance Fee Scheme

An advance fee scheme occurs when the victim pays money to someone in anticipation of receiving something of greater value, such as a loan, contract, investment, or gift, and then receives little or nothing in return.

The variety of advance fee schemes is limited only by the imagination of the con artists who offer them. They may involve the sale of products or services, the offering of investments, lottery winnings, and found money.

Con artists will offer to find financing arrangements for their clients who pay a finder's fee in advance. They require their clients to sign contracts in which they agree to pay the fee when they are introduced to the financing source. Victims often learn that they are ineligible for financing only after they have paid the finder according to the contract. Such agreements may be legal unless it can be shown that the finder never had the intention or the ability to provide financing for the victims. Some tips to avoid the advanced fee schemes are:

- If the offer appears too good to be true, it is. Follow common business practice. Legitimate business is rarely conducted in cash on a street corner.

- Know who you are dealing with. Depending on the amount of money that you intend to spend, you may want to visit the business location, check with the Better Business Bureau, or consult with your bank, an attorney, or the police.

- Make sure you fully understand any business agreement that you enter into. If the terms are complex, have them reviewed by an attorney.

- Be wary of businesses that operate out of post office boxes or mail drops. Do not deal with persons who do not have a direct telephone line, or who are never in when you call, but always return your call later.

- Be wary of business deals that require you to sign non-disclosure or non-circumvention agreements that are designed to prevent you from independently verifying the bona fides of the people with whom you intend to do business. Con artists often use non-circumvention agreements to threaten their victims with civil suit if they report their losses to law enforcement.

Common Health Insurance Frauds

Medical Equipment Fraud: Equipment manufacturers offer free products to individuals. Insurers are then charged for products that were not needed or delivered.

Rolling Lab Schemes: Fake tests are given to individuals at health clubs, retirement homes, or shopping malls and billed to insurance companies or Medicare.

Services Not Performed: Customers or providers bill insurers for services never rendered by changing bills or submitting fake ones.

Medicare Fraud: Any of the health insurance frauds described above. Senior citizens are targets of Medicare schemes, especially by medical equipment manufacturers who offer seniors free medical products in exchange for their Medicare numbers. Because a physician has to sign a form certifying that equipment or testing is needed before Medicare pays for it, con artists fake signatures or bribe doctors to sign the forms. After a signature is in place, the manufacturers bill Medicare for merchandise or service that was not needed or ordered.

Here are some tips to avoid the health insurance fraud:

- Never sign blank insurance claim forms.

- Never give blanket authorization to a medical provider to bill for services rendered.

- Ask your medical providers what they will charge and what you will be expected to pay out-of-pocket.

- Carefully review your insurer's explanation of the benefits statement. Call your insurer and provider if you have questions.

- Do not do business with door-to-door or telephone salespeople who tell you that services of medical equipment are free.

- Give your insurance or Medicare identification only to those who have provided you with medical services.

- Keep accurate records of all health care appointments.

- Know if your physician ordered equipment for you.

Prime Bank Note

International fraud artists have invented an investment scheme that offers extremely high yields in a relatively short time. They purport to have access to bank guarantees which they can buy at a discount and sell at a premium. By reselling the bank guarantees several times, they claim to be able to produce exceptional returns on investment.

If $10 million worth of bank guarantees can be sold at a 2 percent profit on 10 separate occasions, or traunches, the seller would receive a 20 percent profit. Such a scheme is often referred to as a "roll program."

To make their schemes more enticing, con artists often refer to the guarantees as being issued by the world's Prime Banks. Official sounding terms are used: Prime Bank Guarantees, Prime Bank Notes, and Prime Bank Debentures.

Legal documents associated with such schemes often require the victim to enter into non-disclosure and non-circumvention agreements, and offer returns on investment in "a year and a day," and claim to use forms required by the International Chamber of Commerce (ICC). The ICC has issued a warning to all potential investors that no such investments exist.

The purpose of these frauds is to encourage the victim to send money to a foreign bank where it is eventually transferred to an offshore account that is in the control of the con artist. From there, the victim's money is used for the perpetrator's personal expenses or is laundered.

While foreign banks use instruments called bank guarantees in the same manner that U.S. banks use letters of credit to insure payment for goods in international trade, such bank guarantees are never traded or sold on any kind of market. Some tips to avoid prime bank note related fraud are:

- Be wary of an investment referred to as a "roll program" that offers unusually high yields by buying and selling anything issued by Prime Banks.

- Verify the identity of the people involved, the veracity of the deal, and the existence of the security in which you plan to invest.

- Be wary of business deals that require non-disclosure or non-circumvention agreements that are designed to prevent you from verifying information about the investment.

Other Investment Scams To Watch Out For

High Yield Interest Programs Using "Off Sheet Financing"

If you hear the words "post-World War II Bretton Woods," "off-sheet financing," "Top 50 worldwide banks," and "guaranteed or risk-free trading" at the same time, turn tail and run. These scammers will tell you that they are one of only a few traders in the world who know about this venture. They will then tell you that you often need $100 million dollars just to get started, but at this time you can get started with just a small amount or you can pool your money with your friends' money to get up to the $100 million mark.

Then they tell you that those that have done these trades have secretly made hundreds of millions of dollars (no government knowledge, no taxes). Then they claim that they are letting you in on it because they have made enough for themselves and want to see others make money, too. They will tell you that there is no way that your money can disappear, and that it will sit in your own bank account unmolested until your hundreds of millions arrive. They will tell you that you can make astronomical interest rates, such as 20 percent to 80 percent per week, and that exponentially your profits will skyrocket.

Then they ask you to deposit your money in an account with a Prime Bank such as Citibank, CreditSuisse, or in a safe-deposit box. If you have placed your money into one of the banks, the scam artists forge a letter of credit which they then exercise and transfer your money offshore. If you put your money into a safety deposit box, they convince you to buy a bond to earn interest on that money instead of just having it sit there. Of course, the bond is simply one that they made up. Anyway you look at it, your money is gone.

Costa Rica Property Scams

A real estate agent brings you to Costa Rica and persuades you to buy property for your retirement. The problem is that you assume that Costa Rica has laws similar to the U.S., but in Costa Rica, there are squatter's rights. After a person is on your property, you have no legal right to remove them. The only way to do it is to pay them to move.

When you come back to claim your land, the real estate agent has moved squatters onto your property and now there is nothing you can do about it according to the law. The agent then offers to buy back the property as a token of kindness, but only offers about 10 percent since the property now has no value.

CASE STUDY: KENNETH LONG

In my business, I have seen many different financial mistakes. Most of them are common knowledge, such as keeping up with credit card payments. Although credit card issuers frequently forgive a late payment as a one-time courtesy, doing so repeatedly can send their credit score plunging for years to come. Other mistakes are waiting too late to start saving, investing in ways that lead to extreme risk, getting too much consumer debt, or buying more home than you need.

A terribly sad investment mistake is to fall victim to a scam.

The worst scam situation I ever handled dealt with a senior citizen living on social security and a small retirement fund. She received a letter stating that she won the lottery. She was unaware that this was a common fraud. She promptly sent over $3000 to pay for the taxes on the money she won, not knowing that winners never have to pay taxes on lottery proceeds out of pocket.

As if this was not bad enough, she then received a phone call originating from an unregistered cellular phone in Canada. The caller had good news and informed her that, due to another winner not coming forward, she had won double the amount explained to her in the letter. Again, following his instructions, she sent in another payment to cover taxes on the additional winnings.

CASE STUDY: KENNETH LONG

By the time she realized that there was something wrong, she had lost nearly $7000 from her retirement fund. Law enforcement officials had to inform her that not only was her money lost for good, but that there was little chance of ever finding the culprit and bringing him to justice.

Following the right financial steps, on the other hand, will pay off. The best piece of advice that I can give, and one that any good advisor will give, is to start saving early and often. It pays to put aside a small amount early so that your money works for you. Waiting just five or six years to begin can cut your retirement benefits in half. Many people have to overcompensate later in life just trying to catch up. They do this without the benefit of time to help their money grow. Even low wage earners can retire as millionaires.

One of my colleagues worked with a long-time janitor of a major computer company. This janitor found out he had made some good choices, albeit unknowingly.

When he started as a janitor in the company, he signed some financial documents concerning retirement. He did not truly understand what they meant, but he did know that working towards retirement was beneficial. He signed. Without realizing what he was doing, that signature began his retirement plan with a company that would grow into a global entity.

Many years later, he discovered that he was worth more than the people he cleaned up after. He found out that those papers he signed so long ago meant that he had over $1 million in retirement savings. Not bad for a man who never made more than meager wages. He decided to hang up his mop for good.

Everyone has the opportunity to have their own good financial story, just as they can have the prospect of having a poor one. The difference

CASE STUDY: KENNETH LONG

between the two is understanding good and bad financial choices. The best way to understand is to hire a good financial planner.

Kenneth Long

President

Fiscal Progress

Phone: 919-719-1750

Fax: 866-230-7495

Website: www.fiscalprogress.org

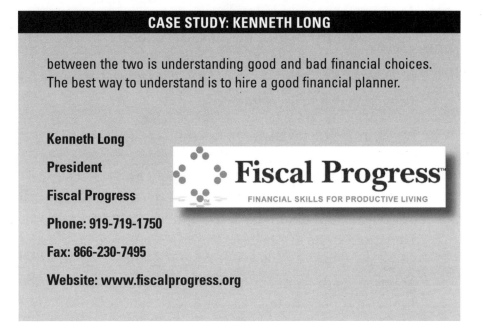

How to Keep From Getting Ripped Off

The following is a 10-point system to staying out of trouble:

1. **Trust your gut instincts.** If an investment sounds too good to be true, it often is and you should politely decline to pursue it.

2. **Run it by advisors you trust.** Before making an investment, run it by your trusted advisors such as your Comprehensive Financial Advisor, your CPA, your attorney, and your spouse.

3. **Only invest with member firms** of the National Association of Securities Dealers (NASD) and Securities Investors Protection Corporation (SIPC). If buying securities, only do business with investment companies that are members of the NASD and the SIPC.

4. **If a security is not publicly traded, do not buy it**. Never buy a security that is not already publicly traded with a verifiable history. Never buy a private placement, limited partnership, precious metal, viatical settlement or promissory note investment.

5. **Never buy any investment over the phone.**

6. **Get the brokers' license number and check their background**. Ask if the investment broker is licensed with the NASD and obtain his CID number and then check his background by contacting the NASD public disclosure program at 800-289-9999 or 301-590-6500, on the Internet at **www.nasdr.com**. You will be able to learn how long the broker has been in business and what complaints (if any) are on his record.

7. **If buying insurance, verify it is licensed for sale in your state**. If you are buying insurance verify both the product and the broker selling it are licensed with your state department of insurance or insurance commissioner. You can reach this department by contacting directory assistance in your state capital. Or you can locate your state insurance commissioner information from the National Association of Insurance Commissioners at (816) 783-8500 or on the Internet at **www.naic.org**.

8. **Check the financial ratings.** If you are buying insurance, verify the insurance carriers financial strength rating from the major rating agencies: A.M. Best, Duff & Phelps, & Standard & Poors.

9. **Use restrictive endorsements.** When buying an investment, always make your check payable to the investment company using a restrictive endorsement. If you are opening an account with ABC brokerage and your

name is John Smith you would style your check as follows: "ABC Brokerage FBO John Smith." The letters FBO stand for "For the Benefit Of" which means that it can only be deposited into your account at ABC Brokerage. Never make your investment check payable to the individual selling the reinvestment and never invest using cash.

10. **Get it in writing.** Get a copy of everything you sign and all account-opening documents, prospectuses, and product disclosures.

W.C. Field once said, "You cannot cheat an honest man."

As Roland Barach has elaborated:

"No honest man will be lured by greed into shady deals. It is also often true that you cannot cheat a person who is looking for an 'honest' profit since such a person will be keeping his eyes open and will examine the entire financial picture.

"It is when we are looking for the 'dishonest' large return that greed blinds us to the dangers involved. At such times we forget the famous admonition that warns us, 'If it is too good to be true, then it often is.'

"The honest man, like the dishonest man, feels greed, but he sticks to certain standards. It is the willingness to abandon those standards that makes some people criminals, and it is the willingness to abandon standards of prudence and reasonable expectations of profits that can cause the financial downfall of the average investor."

The bottom line on scams is to the use common sense, not to let greed trick you into a foolish investment, and do your homework before buying anything.

The next chapter explains in more detail how different investment vehicles work, and how you can make them work to help you have an income retirement. It is just an overview and you should always seek professional advice before following any advice found in a book.

NOW YOU KNOW
1. It is very difficult to get your money back if you have been cheated over the phone.
2. If you receive a letter from Nigeria asking you to send personal or banking information, do not reply in any manner. Send the letter to the U.S. Secret Service or the FBI.
3. Identity fraud occurs when someone assumes your identity for criminal purposes.
4. The variety of advance fee schemes is limited only by the imagination of the con artists who offer them. They may involve the sale of products or services, the offering of investments, lottery winnings, and found money.
5. Give your insurance and Medicare identification only to those who have provided you with medical services.
6. While foreign banks use instruments called bank guarantees in the same manner that U.S. banks use letters of credit to insure payment for goods in international trade, such bank guarantees are never traded or sold on any kind of market.
7. If you hear the words "post-World War II Bretton Woods", "off-sheet financing," "Top 50 worldwide banks," and "guaranteed or risk-free trading," run.
8. Real estate laws are different in each country.

CHAPTER 15:
Creating Fixed Income

The goal of this chapter is to use typical investment vehicles, stocks and bonds, to create residual income.

DEFINITION:	Residual income is income that continues to flow even after you have provided a product or service. The simplest way to think of residual income is "do the work once, get paid forever."

Laddering Your Stocks

DEFINITION:	The cash flow associated with stocks is dividends.

Dividends are paid quarterly. Many people think of quarterly and assume that means March, June, September, and December. Not all stocks pay at that time. That is why you should look for laddered stocks, which pay at different times. To have monthly income, you will need a stock that pays a dividend every month. Below is an example of a laddered stock portfolio.

Payable			
Date	Company	Number of Stock Held	Dividend Amount
01/25/00	General Electric	1000	$102.50
02/15/00	Clorox	250	$104.50
03/12/00	3M	200	$109.50
04/25/00	General Electric	1000	$102.50
05/15/00	Clorox	250	$104.50
06/12/00	3M	200	$109.50
07/25/00	General Electric	3000 (3 to 1 stock split)	$102.50
08/15/00	Clorox	250	$104.50
09/12/00	3M	200	$109.50
10/25/00	General Electric	3000	$102.50
11/15/00	Clorox	250	$104.50
12/12/00	3M	200	$109.50

Consider the effect of this over time.

You buy 100 shares of GE at $100 per share, for $10,000. You collect $307.50 in dividends in the first year. Ten years later, if the dividend has grown to $4.34, you will be collecting $435 in dividends on that $10,000 investment. In another 10 years, if the dividend continues to grow at 12 percent, it'll be $13.50 per share, or $1,350 for you. See what has happened? Buying and holding now reward you with a 13.5 percent (and growing) annual dividend, and that is ignoring any stock price appreciation.

CD Ladder

A CD ladder takes advantage of interest rates spread over several maturities without sacrificing liquidity. Suppose you have $20,000 to invest in CDs. A traditional CD ladder would be for five years and it would have five rungs: one-year, two-year, until you reach the five-year CD. You could invest $4,000 in each rung. After one year, the first CD matures and the others move down a year. The two-year CD is now due in one year; the three-year CD is due in two years, and on down the line. The money from the CD that has just matured is rolled over into a five-year CD. Each year you replace the rung that is farthest out.

The purpose of a CD ladder is to eliminate the emotional decision-making that goes on within an investment or savings plan while evening out the highs and lows that come with interest rate cycles. You are only reinvesting a portion of it when yields are real low. That balances with the times you reinvested at a high rate of return. Over time the ladder smoothes out the peaks and valleys.

When interest rates are low, you should keep the ladder short. Establish shorter maturities now, three months, six months, and one year. As money matures and yields begin to rebound, take larger steps and invest in the longer maturities.

When laddering a portfolio of CDs, make sure the maturities match your cash needs. It is great rolling over CDs and their interest, but it is more important that your money is liquid when you need it. Penalties will seriously crunch your returns. While a five-year ladder will allow you to take advantage of the best interest rates offered, your ladder could be shorter if it makes you more comfortable. Likewise, the rungs should be whatever maturities suit your liquidity needs. The following is an example of how laddering your CDs is better than putting all your money into a particular maturity:

Investor "A" bought a $50,000 one-year CD and reinvested in one-year CDs every year thereafter at the following rates:

Investor "A" — Reinvesting plan	
Year	Rate
Initial purchase	5.85 percent
End of year 1	6.10 percent
End of year 2	5.60 percent
End of year 3	5.05 percent
End of year 4	6.50 percent
End of year 5	4 percent

204 THE COMPLETE PERSONAL FINANCE BOOK

Investor "B" bought $10,000 each of a one-, two-, three-, four- and five-year CDs in May 1998, and then bought $10,000 five-year CDs as each CD matured. The CD rates are:

Investor "B" — Laddered Portfolio	
Initial Investment	Buy When Initial CD Matures
1 year @ 5.85 percent	5 years @ 7.10 percent
2 years @ 6.40 percent	5 years @ 6.20 percent
3 years @ 6.70 percent	5 years @ 5.95 percent
4 years @ 6.90 percent	5 years @ 7.20 percent
5 years @ 7.10 percent	5 years @ 5.45 percent

Compare the annual income stream from these two strategies.

Income Comparison: Reinvesting Versus Laddered Portfolio							
	Year 1	Year 2	Year 3	Year 4	Year 5	This year	Total income
Investor A	$2,925	$3,050	$2,800	$2,525	$3,250	$2,000	$16,550
Investor B	$3,295	$3,420	$3,400	$3,190	$3,325	$3.355	$19,985

The laddered-CD plan (Investor B) returned $3,435 more interest income during the six-year period. The plan also provided a steadier stream of income. Investor "A's" income fluctuated as much as $1,250 between the best and worst years, whereas Investor B's income only fluctuated $230. In a normal yield curve, longer-term maturities will often have higher yields than shorter-term maturities.

DRIPS

Now let us look at DRIPS since this takes little initial capital to get involved in the stock market.

DEFINITION:	The word "DRIP" is an acronym for "dividend reinvestment plan," but "DRIP" also happens to describe the way the plan works. With DRIPs, the dividends that an investor receives from a company go toward the purchase of more stock, making the investment in the company grow little by little.

With a DRIP: You have physical possession of at least one stock certificate.

What is so special about these methods? DRIPS allow you to debit an account and automatically invest in that stock with no commission. With the traditional method of stock acquisition you can buy a minimum of one stock. If a stock is $100 a share, after you own a full stock, the DRIP would allow you to invest $25 and purchase a percentage rather than have to get the entire share. DRIPS also allow you to reinvest the dividends that are paid back into the stock on a quarterly basis with no commission.

Using Bonds for Residual Income

Besides returning the principal, most bonds guarantee payment of interest at a specified rate. The rate of interest on the face amount (par) is referred to as the coupon rate or interest rate. Bonds often pay twice a year; you need six bonds with laddered maturity dates.

Another example using Treasury Bonds: Professionals acknowledge that Treasury bonds are the most dependable investment—the one means of ensuring that assets will always grow. Yet recommending them often triggers two negative thoughts: low returns and inflation risk.

Here is a Treasury bond strategy that protects against inflation; it demonstrates that the strategy has provided impressive asset growth over time. Individual investors can buy bonds directly from the U.S. Treasury on line at **www.treasurydirect.gov** or by phone at 1-800-722-2678. No trading fees or any other fees are charged, and the Treasury will maintain your account with no management fee. Dealing directly with the Treasury can put you 50 basis points ahead of a typical Treasury-bond mutual fund. That is $5 more in your account, annually, for every $1,000 invested.

206 THE COMPLETE PERSONAL FINANCE BOOK

Here is the approach you can use: it is known as a laddered-bond strategy. With $1,000 you buy a 10-year Treasury bond; the current yield is about 4 percent. At the end of the year, your account will show the bond at its face value—$1,000—plus the interest you have received—about $40.

Next year, when your first bond is a year closer to maturity, you invest $1,000 in a new 10-year Treasury bond. Now here is the inflation protection that this strategy offers. The interest offered on the new bond will be different from the roughly four percent paid this year. The difference will result from a number of factors, but the most important is inflation. If inflation is rising, you will receive more than four percent; if it is falling, you will receive less.

Over time, the strategy will keep up with changes in inflation. In periods when inflation and interest rates are rising, the value of your assets may fall behind, because you already own bonds with lower interest payments. But you will catch up in periods of falling inflation because all the bonds you own will pay interest that is higher than the interest rates on new bonds.

At the end of the second year, your account will show $2,000 in face value for the two bonds you bought, plus $80 in interest from the first bond and, say $38 dollars of interest from the second bond for a total of $2,118. What is important is that you will own one Treasury bond at that point that will be paid off in eight years and a second bond that will be paid off in nine years.

If you buy a third bond at the beginning of the third year, you will then own bonds that will be paid off in eight, nine, and ten years. At the end of ten years, your portfolio will contain ten bonds, one of which will be paid off in each of the following ten years. In the eleventh year, the first bond you bought will be paid off, and if you contribute another $1,000 to your account, you will have $2,000 (plus accumulated interest) to invest in a new

10 year Treasury bond. If you continue the strategy through 20 years, then with the same $1,000 of annual contributions you will be buying more than $3000 of a new bond every year.

Asset Growth: Laddered 10-year Treasury Bonds		
$1,000 invested each year -- Profits and Interest reinvested		
	Total Invested	Ending Assets
1940-2002	$63,000.	$790,032.
1940-1960	21,000.	26,922.
1961-1980	20,000.	38,820.
1981-2002	22,000.	62,214.
1997-2002	6,000.	7,533.

A ladder may also be constructed of municipal bonds, but that would often require a minimum of $100,000 in capital to gather a diversified group of issues. Trading in municipal bonds ("munies"), which you can do through most brokerage firms, also creates higher transaction costs, but if your tax rate is high enough—anything above 25 percent—the tax savings will likely make the costs worthwhile.

Residual income is incremental. You need to search for several different ways to generate income and no one way will cover all your needs. While you are still building up your cash flow, reinvest that interest into your mutual fund or annuity and watch your money continue to grow.

If you want to create a residual income, you have to stick with the program. Do your predictable savings. Use the type of investments instruments that I am talking about as you get started and do not attempt the exotic stuff.

Taxes affect many areas of your life, including investing, retirement, and simply earning income. Reading Chapter Fifteen will give you a tax overview. Remember, getting advice from a CPA is crucial since tax laws can change yearly.

CASE STUDY: SUE

Sue was a recent widow. She never managed any of her money while her husband was alive. All the money, $1.5 million, was in a brokerage firm and had been there for ten years. When her husband died, she sat down with the broker to find out what to do next.

Her broker told her that she did not need to worry about how much she took out of the portfolio. She believed him. She began taking out $11,000 to $12,000 a month—10 percent of her portfolio. By the time the crunch of 2000 came, she was down to half the original principal.

It was then that she went to a financial advisor. The only real advice at that point was to cut down on expenses, move into a condo to lower living expenses, and go back to work. This advisor explained that she could take no more than 4 percent of her portfolio for living.

If her broker had told her the same thing, she would have been taking out about $60,000.

She did not realize that she was trying to live off her residual income, and her broker did not explain it to her. Her broker was not an advisor.

He did not know her entire financial situation. He did not know all her assets and liabilities. He did not know her long-term goals, and his advice caused her to lose money and peace of mind.

NOW YOU KNOW
1. Residual income is incremental. You need to be searching for several different ways to generate income, and no one way will cover all your needs.
2. Laddered stocks pay at different times. If you have one that pays in March and then quarterly, you also need to find stocks that pay January and quarterly, and February and quarterly.
3. The most important thing to remember when laddering a portfolio of CDs is to make sure the maturities match your cash needs.
4. You should always look at a company rating and stay away from junk bonds.

CHAPTER 16:
Taxes—What You Should Know

The purpose of tax planning is to take advantage of the available opportunities under current laws to reduce the amount of income taxes owed. Congress has created certain tax loopholes for incentive purposes, such as investing in business property or exploring for gas and oil. There is nothing illegal or immoral connected with using such loopholes.

Tax Reduction IS Legal

Three terms should be defined at this time:

- Tax evasion refers to an illegal, fraudulent act of misreporting facts to the government. It often consists of not filing a tax return, understating income, or overstating expenses and deductions. It is a serious federal offense and is punishable by heavy fines and imprisonment.

- Tax deferral refers to delaying payment of tax to a later time. Tax deferral provides a benefit based on the time value of money. As a result, $1,000 received today is worth more than $1,000 received a year from now since this money accrues interest during the year. Inflation makes the time value of money even more important. For this reason, tax deferrals are an integral part of tax planning techniques.

- Tax reduction refers to a payment lowering of the income tax owed. Tax reduction is therefore the most advantageous result of income tax planning.

While tax planning must exclude any thought of tax evasion, it should encompass the legal techniques of tax deferral and tax reduction. The time, effort, and money put into tax planning will provide benefits that far exceed the cost. The goal here is to focus on those tax reduction and avoidance strategies that will help you increase cash flow today.

Income Taxes and Tax Reduction

If you are getting an income tax refund, do not be happy. The government is robbing you of cash flow and creating an opportunity cost the amount of income you give up by allowing someone else, in this case, the government, to control your money.

Flexible Spending Arrangements (FSA)

DEFINITION:	A Flexible Spending Account (FSA) is an employee benefit program that allows you to set aside money on a pre-tax basis for eligible health care expenses not reimbursed by any medical, dental, or vision care plan. This includes deductibles, co-payments, and other non-covered expenses.

An FSA is a good way to pay for medical expenses with pre-tax dollars. Under this program, you reduce your taxable income by transferring a portion of your salary into a separate account set up by your employer. As you incur medical or dental expenses, the fund reimburses you.

If you make $30,000 a year and put $2,000 into your FSA, your taxable income is $28,000.

Timing Your Capital Gains Tax

DEFINITION: A simple definition for capital gains tax would be a tax levied on the profits you make from the sale, transfer or giving away of any asset. This asset could be anything from a house to timber.

If you plan the sale of an investment property on which capital gains tax will be payable, consider deferring the sale until after December 31. This defers payment of the tax for 12 months. The potential benefit is enhanced if your income will be substantially lower in the following year, perhaps because you are retiring or reducing your workload.

Catch Up on Your 401(k) or IRA Contributions

Some plans allow you to catch up on the maximum allowed contributions in December. This is a good way to reduce your taxes. It is even better if your company matches funds.

Claim Additional Withholding

Another way is by claiming additional withholding on your W-4. You may claim withholding allowances for the following:

1. Moving expense deduction

2. Contributions to IRA accounts

3. Estimated net losses from:

- Business (Schedule C)

- Capital Losses (Schedule D)

- Supplemental Income (Schedule E)

- Farm Losses (Schedule F)

4. Deduction for employee travel expenses and outside salespersons expenses

5. Itemized deductions

You may be entitled to one or more income tax deductions if you provide more than half of your elderly relative's financial support by claiming them as a dependent on your federal income taxes, deducting some of their medical expenses, and modifications on your home needed for appropriate elder care.

Suppose you get a $1,000 refund. That means $83 a month was loaned interest free to the IRS. By the time you receive the refund in May or June, you have paid another five or six months of $83 payments, or $415.

Here is what you do: adjust your W-4 to stop the $83 a month withholding and put the money into an IRA or a 401(k) plan. By doing this for a full year, you add $1,000 into your plan, and get a $350 tax break.

Add it up. You have $1,000 cash in your tax-deferred plan, you have earned $50 on your savings, and you have protected $415 cash from further withholding. That makes your total benefit around $1,815, or more than three times the real value of your refund.

Check with your accountant to see what further allowances you can take to create more cash flow and allow the government to use less of your money for free.

Other Techniques

- **Donations.** When preparing your federal tax return, do not forget to count contributions to charitable organizations. Your donations can add up to a nice tax deduction if you itemize on Form 1040, Schedule A. If you donate $500 worth of clothes and household goods to a charity, and you are in the 28 percent tax bracket, you will add another tax savings of $140.

- **Convert personal debt to mortgage debt.** Mortgage debt is tax deductible—personal debt is not. If you have personal debt of $22,000 in car loans and credit cards and currently have a mortgage of $70,000, increasing your mortgage loan to $92,000 at the same rate of interest will only increase your monthly mortgage payments by $50 and increase your mortgage interest $2,500. The increase of mortgage interest at a 28 percent tax bracket will provide a tax savings of $700. Additionally, you will lose your personal debt payments, say $700, and only increase your mortgage by $50. That is $650 per month you can now use to create another stream of income.

Income Taxes and Tax Credits

DEFINITION: Unlike a tax deduction that only reduces the amount of your taxable income, a tax credit reduces the amount of tax you owe.

Credits are often more powerful than deductions. A tax deduction of $1,000 in the 28 percent tax bracket saves you $280 in taxes. A tax credit will save you the full $1,000. It is a dollar-for-dollar offset. Here is a list of some tax credits to be aware of. (Warning: This is not a complete list and you will want to consult with your CPA before using these credits.)

1. Child Tax Credit

2. Hope Scholarship Credit

3. Lifetime Learning Credit

4. Earned Income Credit

5. Child/Dependent Care Credit

6. General Business Credit

7. Elderly or Disabled Credit

8. Alternative Energy Vehicle Credit

9. Disabled Access Credit

10. Foreign Tax Credit

Investment Tax Earnings and Divorce

You can make unlimited tax-free transfers of investment assets held in taxable accounts between you and your spouse while you are still married. The same is true for transfers between you and your ex-spouse as long as they are made according to the divorce settlement.

If your divorce settlement states that you are to pay a portion of your XYZ stock shares to your ex-spouse, there is no tax impact at the time of that transfer. Your ex-spouse gets those shares and starts exactly where you left off. He will be under the same tax rules that would apply if you still owned the stock. When your ex sells, he or she will owe the federal capital gains tax (typically 15 percent) plus any state and local taxes.

After a divorce, if you own appreciated investments, you will end up with higher taxes. Sometimes, depending on the tax figures, you would be better off with non-appreciated assets, such as cash or actual items like furniture. If you want to split investments evenly, you will need to take this tax liability into account. Use the net value of the appreciated investments after tax to help determine the 50/50 split.

If you make transfers after the divorce, you have to be careful. Any transfers within the first year are considered incident to divorce, meaning they are happening as a result of the divorce. If you make transfers past the one-year mark, you must show that they are related to the divorce. After six years, the option to transfer tax-free is eliminated.

Splitting up a retirement account in a divorce can be tricky. The split needs to happen via a qualified domestic relations order (QDRO) that explains that the ex-spouse will legally receive a right to a specified portion of your retirement plan's balance or benefit payments. Since your ex-spouse is entitled to this money, he or she will also be responsible for paying related taxes when it is time to withdraw these funds at retirement.

The QDRO may also state that ex-spouses may take their share and roll it over into their own IRA without tax implications at the time of the roll over. With withdrawal at retirement, ex-spouses will be required to pay the appropriate taxes.

If your retirement account money goes to your ex-spouse without a QDRO, the money is treated as a taxable distribution to you, and you end up owing the IRS for money that you no longer have. On top of that, you will also end up with the 10 percent premature withdrawal penalty if you are under 59-1/2.

Do not assume that your divorce lawyer will understand all the tax implications when splitting a retirement fund. Consult a tax professional who deals extensively with divorce cases.

You will not need a QDRO to split up your IRA accounts, but be careful. You can roll over money tax-free from your IRA to your ex-spouse's IRA if your divorce property settlement calls for the transfer. Then the ex-spouse can manage his/her IRA and defer taxes until money is withdrawn. At that point, the ex-spouse, not you, will owe the taxes.

Make sure your divorce papers include the following words: "Any division of property accomplished or facilitated by any transfer of IRA or SEP account funds from one spouse or ex-spouse to the other is deemed to be made pursuant to this divorce settlement and is intended to be tax-free under Section 408(d)(6) of the Internal Revenue Code." If money from an IRA account set up in your name gets into your spouse or ex-spouse's hands in any other fashion, you are on the hook for any taxes. You will owe the 10 percent penalty if this happens before you are 59-1/2. This amounts to a tax-free windfall for your ex-spouse at your expense. The same rules apply to simplified employee pension (SEP) accounts, because they are treated as IRAs for this purpose.

These are just a few tax tips. Whatever you save in taxes, you should be spending on wealth creation. For further information, speak to your financial advisor.

NOW YOU KNOW
1. While tax planning must exclude any thought of tax evasion, it should encompass the legal techniques of tax deferral and tax reduction.
2. Check with your accountant to see what allowances you can take to create more cash flow while reducing your year-end tax return. It is better to have the money now and use it wisely than lend it to the government with no interest.
3. Credits are often more powerful than deductions. A tax deduction of $1,000 in the 28 percent tax bracket saves you $280 in taxes. A tax credit will save you the full $1000. It is a dollar-for-dollar offset.
4. Life events, such as divorce, can cause tax turmoil if not dealt with correctly. Seek advice from a CPA or tax lawyer.

Appendix A:
Budget & Saving

Guess Your Expenditures

Many people incorrectly guess what their monthly expenditures are in such areas as food and electricity. See how you do. Put in your guess and then look at your checkbook, debit card statement, and receipts to tally the real figure. How close were you?

Item	Your Guess	Real Amount
Groceries		
Electric and Other Utilities		
Eating Out		
Movies		
Gasoline		
Personal Hygiene Items		
Household Items other than food		
Car Repairs		
Clothes, Shoes, Accessories		

Budget Worksheet

A budget is necessary to turn your dreams into a reality. You have to know what you are making and what you are spending. Each item on your budget needs to be listed. Hoping that you can make ends meet will not make you financially secure and will keep you from buying that home or retiring comfortably.

CATEGORY	BUDGET AMOUNT
INCOME (after taxes):	
Wages and Bonuses	
Interest Income	
Investment Income	
Miscellaneous Income	
Income Total	
EXPENSES:	
HOME (Fixed):	
Mortgage or Rent	
Homeowners/Renters Insurance	
Property Taxes	
HOA Dues	
HOME (Variable):	
Home Repairs	
Maintenance	
UTILITIES (Variable):	
Electricity	
Water and Sewer	
Natural Gas or Oil	
Telephone (Land Line, Cell)	
FOOD (Variable):	
Groceries	
FAMILY OBLIGATIONS (Fixed):	
Child Support/Alimony	
Day Care, Babysitting	

CATEGORY	BUDGET AMOUNT
Church Tithing	
HEALTH AND MEDICAL (Fixed):	
Insurance (medical, dental, vision)	
HEALTH AND MEDICAL (Variable):	
Out-of-Pocket Medical Expenses	
TRANSPORTATION (Fixed):	
Car Payments	
Auto Insurance	
TRANSPORTATION (Variable):	
Auto Repairs/Maintenance/Fees	
Gasoline/Oil	
Other (tolls, bus, subway, taxi)	
DEBT PAYMENTS (Fixed):	
Student Loans	
Other Loans	
DEBT PAYMENTS (Variable):	
Credit Cards	
INVESTMENTS AND SAVINGS (Fixed):	
401(K)or IRA	
Stocks/Bonds/Mutual Funds	
College Fund	
Savings	
Emergency Fund	
MISCELLANEOUS (Variable):	
Toiletries, Household Products	
Grooming (Hair, Make-up, Other)	
Total Monthly Expenses	
Discretionary Funds (Spendable income minus expenses)	

CATEGORY	BUDGET AMOUNT
Home Improvements	
Fitness (Yoga, Massage, Gym)	
Cable TV/Videos/Movies	
Computer Expense	
Hobbies	
Subscriptions and Dues	
Vacations	
Eating Out	
Pet Food	
Pet Grooming, Boarding, Vet	
New Clothing	
Gifts	
Miscellaneous Expense	

College Savings Plan Comparison Chart

	College Savings Plan	Prepaid Tuition Plan	ESA	Savings Bonds
Ownership/ Control	Contributor	Contributor	Contributor	Contributor
Investment Choices	Typically, plans provide several investment options.	None.	No restrictions.	Savings bonds.
Age Limits	None.	Plan may set age or grade limits.	Except for special needs children, no contributions can be made after a child reaches age 18, and withdrawals must be made before beneficiary reaches age 30.	Owner must be at least 24 before the bond's issue date (not purchase date).

	College Savings Plan	Prepaid Tuition Plan	ESA	Savings Bonds
Expenses Covered Besides Tuition & Fees	Qualified education expenses for post-secondary education.	With a few exceptions, only tuition and mandatory fees for post-secondary education are covered.	Qualified elementary and secondary education expenses or qualified higher education expenses.	Tuition and mandatory fees for post-secondary education and contributions to 529s and ESAs.
Contribution Limit	Varies from plan to plan. Majority of plans permit total contributions in excess of $200,000 per beneficiary.	Fixed by terms of contract you purchase.	Contributor: $2,000 per beneficiary per year. Beneficiary: $2,000, does not matter.	No limit.
Federal Tax Advantages	Earnings grow tax-deferred and are tax-free if used for qualified education expenses.	Earnings grow tax-deferred and are tax-free if used for qualified education expenses.	Earnings grow tax-deferred and are tax-free if used for qualified education expenses.	Interest grows tax-deferred and is tax-free if used for qualified education expenses.

	College Savings Plan	Prepaid Tuition Plan	ESA	Savings Bonds
State Tax Advantages	Varies from state to state, but some states provide tax deduction for contributions, tax-free earnings growth, and tax-free withdrawals for qualified education expenses.	Varies from state to state, but some states provide tax-deduction for contributions, tax-free earnings growth, and tax-free withdrawals for qualified education expenses.	None.	Interest is usually tax-exempt from state and local taxes.
Income Phase-Out	None.	None.	Single filers: $95,000-$110,000. Joint filers: $190,000-$220,000.	Single Filers: $61,200-$76,200. Joint Filers: $91,850-$121,850.
Penalties for Non-Qualified Withdrawals	Earnings are taxed as ordinary income and may be subject to 10% penalty.	Earnings are taxed as ordinary income and may be subject to 10% penalty.	None.	Interest earned is taxed as income.

Appendix B:
Basic Banking

How to Balance a Checkbook

Using your statement, and your checkbook/ check register, use the following steps to balance, or reconcile, your checkbook.

STEP 1

In your checkbook, make a checkmark in the appropriate box for each check returned or noted on your statement. In addition, also mark all ATM or other electronic transactions, and all deposits. This way, you will be able to identify all transactions recorded by the bank or financial institution handling your checking account.

Number	Date	Description of Transaction	Payment/Debit		Fee	Deposit/Credit	Balance

STEP 2

Record in your check register any transactions listed on your bank statement that were not recorded in your register. This may include ATM or debit transactions, bank fees, and others.

STEP 3

The back of your bank's statement will often have a checking reconciliation form. Use this form to reconcile your checking account. The form may vary, but often includes the following steps:

A. Write the ending balance shown on your bank statement.

B. Add the total amount of deposits made that were after the ending date of the bank statement (outstanding), and therefore do not appear on the statement. The reconciliation form often has a space where you can list and total these deposits.

C. Subtract the total of any checks still outstanding (checks that you have written that do not show up on your bank statement). The reconciliation form should have a place where you can list and total all outstanding checks.

This amount should then equal the amount listed in your check register or checkbook. If not, you will need to check each of your transactions and also possibly need to check your math.

Basic Banking Fees

Type of Fee	What It Means
Abandoned account	State laws vary, but if your account is dormant for a long time — often three or five years — the bank hands the proceeds to the state, but not before deducting a hefty fee.
Account maintenance fee	Some accounts charge a monthly fee no matter what the balance.
Account closed early	Banks differ, but often if you close an account within 90 or 180 days, you will be charged a fee.
Account research/ reconciliation	This is often a per-hour fee that is charged if there is a discrepancy between your records and the bank's; often the bank will charge a minimum of one hour.
ATM	If you use an ATM that does not belong to your bank, you will be charged a fee by your bank and a surcharge by the owner of the ATM.

Type of Fee	What It Means
ATM/debit card replacement	Lose a card and you may get one new card a year for free if your bank is nice, but you will pay after that.
Check printing	Most accounts charge for checks.
Coin counting	Some banks will not charge customers or children for this service, but most will charge non-customers.
Counter checks	Forget your checkbook or run out of checks? The bank may give you a few for free but charge a fee beyond that.
Credit reference	If you need to rely on the bank for a credit reference, expect to pay.
Debit card	Purchases made with a debit card are deducted from your checking account. Unfortunately, a growing number of banks charge a fee for every purchase.
Deposited item returned (DIR)	If you deposit a check in your account and the check bounces, you will be charged a fee.
Early-withdrawal fee for CDs	Imposed when you close a CD account before maturity.
Inactive account	This monthly or quarterly charge is assessed if you have no deposits or withdrawals over a specific time. Some banks charge if your account has been inactive for as few as 90 days. You may be able to avoid a fee if your balance is above a certain level. Some institutions do not start an inactivity fee until the account has been dormant for one year.

Type of Fee	What It Means
Money orders/ cashier's check	A cashier's check will cost more than a money order.
Monthly service fee	Charged if a checking account balance falls below a certain amount.
Non-sufficient funds (NSF)	Bounce a check and you will pay one of the highest per-item fees banks charge.
Notary fees	A notary public is someone who can certify or attest to documents. If you need something notarized, you will pay a variety of fees depending on the document.
Overdraft	If you overdraw your account and the bank pays the check or debit, it will charge you a fee. The benefit is your check does not bounce and you do not get charged a fee by the business that accepted your check.
Return of checks with statement	You used to be able to get your canceled checks returned for free; now many banks charge a monthly fee for that service.
Safe deposit box	An annual rental fee based on the size of the box.
Stop payment	Imposed when you use a check to pay for something and then change your mind.
Teller fee	Some accounts require you to do most transactions online, at the ATM or by phone. These accounts often limit the number of times you can visit a teller each month and charge a fee for additional visits.

Compound Interest Formula and Example

P is the principal (the initial amount you deposit)
R is the annual rate of interest (percentage)
N is the number of years the amount is deposited or borrowed for.
A is the amount of money accumulated after N years, including interest.

When the interest is compounded once a year:

$$A = P(1 + r)^n$$

So, if you deposit $1,000 and add nothing to it for 30 years at a 10 percent interest rate, your money will have grown to $17,449.40 after 30 years.

$$A = \$1,000(1 + 10\,\%)^{30}$$

Let us suppose you are 20 years old and wish to retire at age 65. What amount of money would you have to deposit at a 10 per cent rate for this one deposit to make you a millionaire?

Here, we know that

- A = $1 million
- N would be 45 (retirement at 65-the current age of 20)
- R is 10 percent
- We are looking for P – the amount of the initial deposit.

$$\$1,000,000 = P\,(1 + 10\,\%)^{45}$$

P, the initial deposit, would be $13,719.21. This shows you the incredible earning power of compound interest.

Appendix C: Insurance

How Much Life Insurance Do I Need?

Life insurance should replace 80 percent of your pretax income:

Current income:_____

Current income times .80: _____

Determine your spouse's monthly social security benefits if you die. This figure can be found on your Social Security statement. Other dependents may also be able to get benefits:

- Spouse who takes care of your child until the youngest turns 16
- Unmarried children until age 18
- Dependent parents over age 62

Monthly Benefits: _____

Yearly Benefits:_____
(Monthly benefits x 12)

Annual Income Insurance Needs to Replace: _____
(Needed income minus Social Security Income)

Total Capital Amount: _____
(Use Table to determine how much you will need based on your annual replacement income AND the number of years to your retirement. This is the amount of insurance you will need.)

Current Annual Income	Years Until You Retire						
	10	15	20	25	30	40	60
$10,000	$92,000	$132,000	$168,000	$201,000	$231,000	$283,000	$361,000
$20,000	$184,000	$263,000	$336,000	$402,000	$461,000	$565,000	$722,000
$30,000	$276,000	$395,000	$504,000	$602,000	$692,000	$848,000	$1,083,000
$40,000	$368,000	$527,000	$672,000	$803,000	$923,000	$1,130,000	$1,444,000
$50,000	$460,000	$659,000	$840,000	$1,004,000	$1,154,000	$1,413,000	$1,805,000
$60,000	$552,000	$790,000	$1,007,000	$1,205,000	$1,384,000	$1,696,000	$2,166,000
$70,000	$643,000	$922,000	$1,175,000	$1,406,000	$1,615,000	$1,978,000	$2,527,000
$80,000	$735,000	$1,054,000	$1,343,000	$1,606,000	$1,846,000	$2,261,000	$2,888,000
$90,000	$827,000	$1,185,000	$1,511,000	$1,807,000	$2,076,000	$2,544,000	$3,249,000
$100,000	$919,000	$1,317,000	$1,679,000	$2,008,000	$2,307,000	$2,826,000	$3,610,000
$110,000	$1,011,000	$1,449,000	$1,847,000	$2,209,000	$2,538,000	$3,109,000	$3,971,000
$120,000	$1,103,000	$1,581,000	$2,015,000	$2,410,000	$2,768,000	$3,391,000	$4,332,000
$130,000	$1,195,000	$1,712,000	$2,183,000	$2,610,000	$2,999,000	$3,674,000	$4,693,000
$140,000	$1,287,000	$1,844,000	$2,351,000	$2,811,000	$3,230,000	$3,957,000	$5,054,000
$150,000	$1,379,000	$1,976,000	$2,519,000	$3,012,000	$3,461,000	$4,239,000	$5,415,000

First Column: Annual income to be replaced. Top Row: Years of replacement income required. Table Body: Lump sum life insurance required. Assumptions: Annual inflation rate assumed to be 4.0%; Annual investment return assumed to be 6.0%.

Other factors to consider:

No emergency fund for the funeral? Add $15,000
Heavy debt? Add amount for debt payoff
No retirement funds? Add an amount to get them started saving for retirement

Final Insurance Needed: _____
(Total Capital Amount plus any other factors)

Example of a Need Life Insurance Form:

Current income: $40,000
Current income times .80: $32,000

Determine your spouse's monthly social security benefits if you die. This can be found on your Social Security statement. Other dependents may also be able to get benefits:

- Spouse who takes care of your child until the youngest turns 16
- Unmarried children until age 18
- Dependent parents over age 62

Monthly Benefits: $2,000

Yearly Benefits: $24,000
(Monthly benefits x 12)

Annual Income Insurance Needs to Replace: $8000
(Needed income minus Social Security Income)

Total Capital Amount: $168,000 Based on $10,000 with 20 years to retirement
(Use Table to determine how much you will need based on your annual replacement income AND the number of years until your retirement. This is the amount of insurance you will need.)

Other factors to consider:

No emergency fund for the funeral? Add $15,000 — have no emergency fund

Heavy debt? Add amount for debt payoff—have $10,000 in debt

No retirement funds? Add an amount to get them started saving for retirement—not needed

Final Insurance Needed: $193,000

$168,000 + $15,000 + $10,000
(Total Capital Amount plus any other factors)

Questions To Ask When Choosing a Long-term Disability Policy

1. What does it cost in monthly/yearly premiums to replace 60 percent of my income? How much will it cost to replace 80 percent of my income?

2. How does your policy handle bonuses, overtime, and commissions? (This is a very important question for someone whose income relies heavily on one or more of these sources. Your policy will need to take into account these items to provide your needed 60 to 80 percent income replacement.)

3. Do you cap income? In other words, is there a maximum amount of disability per month that I am allowed to collect?

4. Does this policy go to age 65?

5. Is this "any occupation" or "own occupation" coverage?

6. How long from becoming disabled until I can receive my first payment? (Six months is better, although one year is much cheaper.)

7. Is the premium guaranteed until age 65? (This means that your insurance premiums cannot be raised. If they say it is "guaranteed renewable" or "a return of premium policy," your premiums are not guaranteed to stay the same.

8. Can I increase my coverage if my income goes up? Can I do so without a medical check up?

9. How does this policy define a disability?

10. What do I have to do to prove that I am unable to work?

11. Is this an accident-only policy? (Do not purchase one of these because they do not cover illnesses.)

How to Lower Your Risk of Identity Theft

If you are following all the guidelines below, you will be at a lower risk from being a victim of identity theft:

- Do you check your credit report annually? This needs to be done to see if there are any signs of fraud. Equifax, Experian, and TransUnion are the bureaus to check and they are required to help you fix problems. You can also request that the credit bureaus put an alert on your credit history to prevent future fraud if you suspect something.

- Do you keep your social security number on your drivers' license or in your wallet? After a criminal has your social security number and all the other information on you driver's license, he has everything he needs. Do not keep your social security number in your wallet, car, or anywhere but a safe place at home and memorize it.

- Do you throw your personal documents out in your trash? The trash is one of the easiest ways to get information from someone. Get a paper shredder or tear everything up in very small pieces and try to distribute in multiple bags to prevent anyone from obtaining personal information or credit card numbers.

- Do you leave bills in the mailbox for the mailman? Leaving bills out by the road waiting for the mailman is like handing a blank check right in the hands of a criminal. Here is what happens: the mail is stolen, the check is cleaned up with some homemade chemicals, and then the criminal has a fresh new check to write to himself. Drop off your bills in a mailbox or directly to the post office instead. In addition, request that your bank hand deliver your statements and canceled checks to you.

- When shopping or transferring personal information online, do you make sure encryption software is used? This software allows your personal information to be sent without hackers' viewing and stealing it. If you are not sure, do not do it. Only use sites that are reputable and that you trust or look for the toll-free number and call in your personal information.

Appendix D: Debt

Excessive Debt Warning Signs Quiz

If you answer yes to three or more questions below, you likely have too much debt. If you answer yes to question 11 through 14 you have a debt problem.

1. You have no savings account.

2. You only make the minimum payment to your credit cards.

3. You use your credit cards for every day items without paying the card in full at the end of the month.

4. You have more than two credit cards.

5. You use 20 percent or more to pay off your debt (excluding your mortgage).

6. You are at your credit limit on your credit cards.

7. You write checks that cannot be covered in hopes that you

will have enough money in your account by the time they clear.

8. You do not know how much you owe.

9. You use your cash advance on your credit cards.

10. You have been declined when making a purchase with your credit card.

11. You cannot get a credit card because of a poor credit rating

12. You habitually bounce checks.

13. Collectors call your home.

14. You lie about your debt or about your spending habits.

Credit Card Reporting Agency Addresses

Equifax Credit Information Services, Inc.
P.O. Box 740241
Atlanta, GA. 30374
1-800-685-1111
www.Equifax.com

TransUnion Corporation
TransUnion LLC
Consumer Disclosure Center
P.O. Box 1000
Chester, PA 19022
1-800-888-4213
www.TransUnion.com

Experian
National Consumer Assistance Center
P.O. Box 949
Allen, TX 75013
1-888-EXPERIAN
www.Experian.com

Remove your name from Credit Bureau mailing that are prepared by the credit bureaus, call 1-888-567-8688 or 1-888-5-OPT-OUT. You can remove your name from the mailing list for a period of two years by phone. To remove your name permanently from the mailing lists, request a form be mailed to you, complete and return it. Calling this one phone number will remove your name from the mailing lists prepared by the three credit bureaus of Equifax, TransUnion, and Experian.

Finding Debt to Income Ratio

Banks will use your total income to determine your debt to income ratio. The fact is that you do not see your total income — you only see your after-tax income. Therefore, you will use that number for this calculation.

Total Bad Debt / After Tax Income = Debt to Income Ratio

Example:

After tax income: $28,732
Total bad debt: $5,237

$5,237 divided by $28,732 equals 18 percent debt to income ratio.

This number is too high. If you have a number above 15 percent, you have too much debt.

Appendix E: Retirement

Retirement Worksheet

Desired Annual Retirement Income (often 80 percent of your current income)	
Add together the following:	
Yearly Social Security benefit	
Yearly Pension	
Post-retirement wages	
Income from other sources	
Income Sources Total	
Subtract the income sources total from the desired annual retirement income. This is how much you will need from savings each year:	
Multiply your needed yearly savings by 25. This is your lifetime retirement expense.	

Adjust for inflation by multiplying your lifetime retirement expense by the inflation factor. Look at the inflation table on the next page to determine the correct factor. This is your adjusted lifetime retirement expense figure.	
How much you need to save:	
Current savings from all sources	
Interest earned from these sources (This can be determined by using the interest table provided in the Retirement Appendices)	
Multiply your current savings by the interest earned. This is your current assets by the time of retirement.	
Find your Gap Factor. This factor takes into account the compounded interest and can be found in the Retirement Appendices	
Multiply your Gap Factor by your savings gap. This gives you the amount you need to save monthly.	

The retirement sheet may make you a bit nervous, but let us look at an example to make you feel a bit more at ease.

Example of the Retirement Worksheet:

Desired Annual Retirement Income (often 80 percent of your current income)	$34,000
Add together the following:	
Yearly Social Security benefit	$18,000
Yearly Pension	$0
Post-retirement wages	$0
Income from other sources	$0
Income Sources Total	$18,000
Subtract the income sources total from the desired annual retirement income. This is how much you will need from savings each year:	$16,000
Multiply your needed yearly savings by 25. This is your lifetime retirement expense.	$400,000
Adjust for inflation by multiplying your lifetime retirement expense by the inflation factor. Look at the inflation table on the next page to determine the correct factor. This is your adjusted lifetime retirement expense figure.	$876,000
How much you need to save:	
Current savings from all sources	$60,000
Interest earned from these sources (This can be determined by using the interest table provided in the Retirement Appendices)	2.19
Multiply your current savings by the interest earned. This is your current assets by the time of retirement.	$131,400
Find your Gap Factor. This factor takes into account the compounded interest and can be found in the Retirement Appendices	$774,600
Multiply your Gap Factor by your savings gap. This gives you the amount you need to save monthly.	$2100.20

As you can see from this example, you are not going to make it by saving alone. You may want to consider working in your retirement, retiring later in life, or being more aggressive with your investment vehicle to earn higher interest.

Given the same amount of savings, if you choose to retire 10 years later, you only need to save $1,576 per month. If you choose to retire in the same 20 years, but expect a 6 percent return on your money, you will only need to save $1,466 per month. If you earn $1,000 a month in a post-retirement job, you only have to save $237.50 per month.

There are many different factors that determine your need for savings each year.

Inflation Factor Table

Inflation Factors for Selected Annual Inflation Rate Over a Number of Years			
Years	3% Inflation Rate	4% Inflation Rate	5% Inflation Rate
5	1.16	1.22	1.28
10	1.34	1.48	1.63
15	1.56	1.80	2.08
20	1.81	2.19	2.65
25	2.09	2.67	3.39
30	2.43	3.24	4.32
35	2.81	3.95	5.52
40	3.26	4.80	7.04

Expected Interest Earned

Expected Rate of Return					
Years Until Retirement	4 percent	6 percent	8 percent	10 percent	11 percent
40	4.80	10.29	21.72	45.26	65
35	3.95	7.69	14.79	28.10	38.57
30	3.24	5.74	10.06	17.45	22.89
25	2.67	4.29	6.85	10.83	13.59
20	2.19	3.21	4.66	6.73	8.06
15	1.80	2.40	3.17	4.18	4.78
10	1.48	1.79	2.16	2.59	2.84
5	1.22	1.34	1.47	1.16	1.69

Gap Factor

	Years							
Return in percent	5	10	15	20	25	30	35	40
2	.016	5	3	3	25	2	15	1
3	.015	7	4	3	2	15	13	1
4	.015	7	4	3	2	15	12	08
5	.014	6	4	25	2	1	09	07
6	.014	6	3	2	15	1	07	05
7	.014	6	3	2	1	1	05	04
8	.013	55	3	15	1	07	04	03
9	.013	5	3	15	08	05	03	02
10	.0125	5	2	1	08	04	03	02
11	.012	5	2	1	06	04	02	01

Comparing a Traditional IRA to a Roth IRA

	Traditional	Roth
Highlights	Savings plan for those who have earned income and are not covered by an employer retirement plan or are covered by an employer retirement plan.	Savings plan with potentially greater tax benefit, such as possible tax-free earnings and no mandatory distribution requirements.
Contribution Limits	2007 $4,000 2008 & beyond $5,000	2007 $4,000 2008 & beyond $5,000
Catch-Up Provisions	Yes: Individuals 50 or older: $1,000	Yes: Individuals 50 or older: $1,000
Tax Deductibility	Possible deductions* - See IRS Publication 590	No
Income Limits	Member must have earned income to contribute. Deductibility is based on annual gross income, and active participation in a retirement plan at work. Single individuals participating in an employer plan earning more than $60,000, and married couples participating in an employer plan earning more than $80,000 will not receive a deduction.	Must have earned income to contribute. However, total income cannot exceed $110,000 for single individuals and $160,000 for married individuals filing a joint tax return. Total annual income cannot exceed $100,000 to complete a conversion from a Traditional IRA to a Roth IRA.

	Traditional	Roth
Penalty-Free Distribution Exceptions	Death, disability, substantial equal periodic payments, first-time home purchase, post-secondary education expenses.	Death, disability, first-time home purchase.
Contributions	Contributions can only be made before the year in which the Member turns 70.	There is no age limit for contribution to a Roth IRA. However, there are income re-quirements.
Distributions	Distributions must be-gin no later than April 1, following the 70th birthday.	Not required to take a mandatory distribution from a Roth IRA.
Contribution Deadline	April 15th (Tax filing deadline, not including extensions).	April 15th (Tax filing deadline, not including extensions).

Appendix F:
Buying A Home

Figuring Out Your Monthly Mortgage Payments

Interest Rate	15 Years	20 Years	30 Years
4.0%	$7.40	$6.06	$4.77
4.5%	$7.65	$6.33	$5.07
5.0%	$7.91	$6.60	$5.37
5.5%	$8.17	$6.88	$5.68
6.0%	$8.44	$7.16	$6.00
6.5%	$8.71	$7.46	$6.32
7.0%	$8.99	$7.75	$6.65
7.5%	$9.27	$8.06	$6.99
8.0%	$9.56	$8.36	$7.34
8.5%	$9.85	$8.68	$7.69
9.0%	$10.14	$9.00	$8.05
9.5%	$10.44	$9.32	$8.41
10.0%	$10.75	$9.65	$8.78

For instance, if you have borrowed $75,000 at 6.5 percent for 30 years, you would find the 6.5 percent row and the 30-year column to find the number $6.32. This means for every $1,000 sold, you will pay $6.32. So, for $75,000, you would pay $474 per month. ($6.32 x 75)

Another example:

- $265,000 loan
- 4 percent
- 20 years

$6.06 per thousand dollars borrowed

$6.06 x 265 = $1,605.90 per month

Finding the Right Home

To find the right home, you will want to look at the following:

Location and Neighborhood

- Suburbs or Country.

  Pros: Often less expensive. Often newer. Tract homes are conforming. More home for the money.

  Cons: More time in traffic if driving to town for work. Farther away from entertainment options cities offer.

- Urban.

  Pros: Closer to many employers. Walking distance to theaters, restaurants, schools. Many period homes offer more distinctiveness in styles.

  Cons: Often noisier. Higher crime rates. More expensive.

- Busy Streets.

  Pros: Often homes on streets with more traffic are thousands of dollars cheaper. If noise does not bother you, do not pass up homes on busy streets. Drive by at different times of the day and week to ascertain noise levels.

  Cons: These types of homes will always sell for less than others in the same area. If bedrooms are located near the front of the home, sleep may be disturbed.

- Cul de sac.

  Pros: Number one choice of buyers with children.

  Cons: Less privacy, neighbors know more about you.

- Corner lots.

  Pros: Often larger lots. Fewer neighbors. More visibility.

  Cons: More traffic noise. More vulnerable to vehicles jumping the curb. Children might trespass at the corner.

Type of Home

- Single Family.

  Pros: Good appreciation. Opportunity for gardens. More privacy. Quieter.

  Cons: More expensive than our next category. More maintenance.

- Condos, Townhomes, Cooperatives.

  Pros: Less expensive than comparable single-family homes. Often newer so fewer repairs. Lock-n-go lifestyle.

No yard or exterior maintenance.

Cons: Less privacy. Noisier. Common walls, floors, and ceilings. Sometimes no private yard or balcony.

Number of Stories

- Single Story.

  Pros: Easy wheelchair access. Easier to clean.

  Cons: Can be noisier if stereos or televisions are located on the same floor as bedrooms. Some people feel safety is compromised if bedrooms are located at ground level. More of the lot is absorbed by living quarters.

- More than One Story.

  Pros: More living space on same foundation than a ranch home. Less noise if entertaining on lower level while other family members sleep upstairs.

  Cons: More trips up and down the stairs to carry stuff to bedrooms. If laundry rooms are on the second floor, washer leaks are major. Might need dual vacuum cleaners. It is difficult to maintain consistent temperatures on each level without dual heating and cooling units.

- **Split Levels.**

  Pros: Often less expensive if purchased with lower level unfinished. Higher ceilings are appealing. Downstairs family room separates noise levels from upstairs. More square footage on same size lots as ranch homes.

  Cons: Less storage space. Hassle to take trash downstairs and carry groceries upstairs or vice versa. Kitchens tend to be smaller.

Interior Specifications

- Number of Bedrooms.

  Pros: Common minimum requested configurations are three bedrooms. Newer parents prefer bedrooms located on one level.

  Cons: Two bedrooms appeal primarily to first-time home buyers, singles or seniors. However, do not discount a two-bedroom if a den will satisfy your space requirements.

- Number of Bathrooms.

  Pros: More than one bath is preferred by most people. One bath homes are often less expensive.

  Cons: Do not pass up a one bath home if there is room to add a second bath. Sometimes it costs less to put in an extra bath than it does to buy a two-bath home.

- Square Footage.

  Pros: larger spaces offer more room and cost less per square foot than smaller spaces.

  Cons: Do not be misled as lay-out is more important than actual square footage. Sometimes well designed smaller spaces appear larger.

- Bonus Rooms.

  Pros: Extra space for media rooms, art studios, children's playrooms, gyms, den/study.

  Cons: More expensive.

- Attached Garage.

Pros: Cheaper to build. Convenient if raining or snowing.

Cons: Higher noise levels inside the home from cars. Some people feel they are an eye sore. If the garage door to the house self locks, you could get locked out at an inopportune time. Your homeowner's insurance rates could be higher because of the danger of spontaneous combustion.

- Detached Garage.

  Pros: Can be tucked away from site lines. Quieter. Cheaper homeowner's insurance rates.

  Cons: More expensive to build. Farther to walk in bad weather.

Additional Considerations

- School districts.

- Special amenities such as fireplaces, pools, or spas.

- Condition of plumbing, electrical, heating, and cooling units.

- Available utilities such as cable, DSL, or satellite.

- Sewer, cesspool, or septic connections.

Should I Use A Real Estate Agent?

With A Real Estate Agent	Without A Real Estate Agent
Real estate agent can find houses for sale in MLS.	You will have to find the houses yourself. If MLS is available to the public in your area, great. If not, you might not be able to find much. Check the list above for tips on finding homes for sale by yourself.
Real estate agent can give a professional opinion of how much a home is worth.	You will pay someone for a professional opinion of value either a CMA from a real estate agent for ~$50, or an appraisal from an appraiser for ~$400. You may have to get an appraisal anyway if you decide to buy the house, with or without a real estate agent.
Real estate agents will not tell you about FSBOs unless the seller is paying a commission to real estate agents.	Every FSBO is an option for you, but you will have to find the properties yourself. Look at ads in the newspaper and ride around the neighborhoods.
Real estate agent will be paid by the seller, often 3 percent of the price of the home.	With no real estate agent, the seller will not have to pay that commission, so you might be able to negotiate a lower price with the seller.

Sample Real Estate Sales Contract

Agreement dated this _____ day of _____ _____by and between_____ _____hereinafter "Seller" whose address is

_____

_____

hereinafter "Buyer" (and/or assigns or nominees) whose address is_____

_____

1. The Property

The parties hereby agree that Seller will sell and Buyer will buy the following property, located in and situated in the County of _____, state of _____, to wit: (legal description) known by street and address as _____

_____.

The sale shall also include all personal property and fixtures, except: _____.

Unless specifically excluded, all other items will be included, whether or not affixed to the property or structures. Seller expressly warrants that property, improvements, building or structures, the appliances, roof, plumbing, heating and/or ventilation systems are in good working order. This clause shall survive closing of title.

2. Purchase Price

The total purchase price to be paid by buyer will be $_____ _____ payable as follows:

Non-refundable earnest money deposit $_____

Balance due at closing $_____

Owner financing from seller $_____

New Loan $_____

Subject to existing loans $_____

Sale price is subject to appraisal by buyer and/or agent of buyer's choice.

3. Earnest Money

The buyer's earnest money shall be held in escrow by agent of buyer's choice. Upon default of this agreement, seller may retain entire sum of earnest money as his sole remedy without further resource between the parties.

4. New Loan

The agreement is contingent upon buyer's ability to obtain a new loan in the amount of $_____.

Buyer is not required to accept any loan with interest rate exceeding _____percent amortized over _____ years or pay any closing costs or points exceeding $_____. Buyer shall provide

seller with written proof of a loan commitment on or before ____ _____, 20 ___.

5. Seller Financing.

Buyer shall execute a promissory note in the amount of $_____ _____. In the case of default by the buyer, recourse shall be against the property and there shall be no personal resource against the borrower. As security for performance of the promissory note, buyer shall provide the seller a mortgage, deed of trust or other customary security agreement which shall be subordinate to a new first mortgage not to exceed $_____.

6. Closing

Closing is to be held be on or about _____, 20_____, at a time and place designed by buyer. Buyer shall choose the escrow, title and/or closing agent. Seller agrees to convey title by a general warranty deed. Parties agree to pursue satisfactory closing with all due diligence.

7. Possession

Seller shall surrender possession to the property in clean condition, and free of all personal items and debris on or before _____ _____, 20_____. (Possession date) In the event possession is not delivered at closing, buyer shall withhold proceeds from the sale in the amount of $_____ as security. Seller shall be liable for damages in the amount of $_____ per day for each day the property is occupied or otherwise unavailable to buyer beyond the possession date. This paragraph shall survive the closing of title.

8. Execution of Terms

This agreement may be executed in counterparts and will be accepted by facsimile signatures. This agreement is in effect as of the date of the last signature.

9. Inspection

The completion of this agreement is subject to the final inspection and approval of the property by the buyer in writing on or before _____, 20_____.

10. Access

Buyer shall be in possession of a key or suitable key code and be entitled to access to show partners, lenders, inspectors and/or contractors prior to closing as needed. Buyer may place an appropriate sign on the property before closing for prospective tenants and/or assigns.

_____   _____

Seller   Date

_____   _____

Seller   Date

_____   _____

Buyer   Date

_____   _____

Buyer   Date

Appendix G: Advisor

Do You Need a Financial Advisor?

Determining whether you need a financial advisor depends on the following items. Each yes answer scores one point. If you have three or more points, you may need an advisor to help you with your finances.

1. I have more than $50,000 in savings, checking, money market, CDs, retirement, and other investments.

2. I use the 1040 form and three or more other forms in order to compute my income taxes.

3. I am not interested in doing financial research.

4. I would rather spend my time on other things than on financial.

5. I am inexperienced when it comes to investing.

6. I have had one of the following happen in the last year:

    a.   Death of a parent

    b.   Got married

    c.   Got divorced

    d.   Bought or sold a house

    e.   Retired

25 Documents to Take With You to Your First Meeting with a Financial Advisor

No matter what kind of financial advisor you see, there are a few key documents that you will need. The following is a list to gather BEFORE meeting with your advisor.

1. Your monthly budget sheet

2. A recent pay stub

3. Last year's tax return

4. Account statement for your pension

5. Account statement for your 401(k)

6. Account statement for your IRA

7. Other retirement account statements

8. Your Social Security statement

9. Checking statement

10. Savings statement

11. Money market statement

12. Brokerage account statement

13. The value of your home

14. The value of other real estate

15. The value of savings bonds

16. The value of stock options

17. The value of any collections such as baseball cards

18. The value of jewelry (only if this goes beyond a few rings and a bracelet or two)

19. Statements showing outstanding debt, including credit cards, mortgages, student loans, consumer loans, auto loans, and home equity loans

20. Declaration page on auto insurance

21. Declaration page on home owner's insurance

22. Declaration page on life insurance

23. Declaration page on disability insurance

24. Declaration page on long-term care insurance

25. Trust fund records

Common Financial Advisor Credentials

AAMS: Accredited Asset Management Specialist

CFA: Chartered Financial Analyst

CFP: Certified Financial Planner

ChFC: Chartered Financial Consultant

CIC: Chartered Investment Counselor

CIMA: Certified Investment Management Analyst

CLU: Chartered Life Underwriter

CM: Certified Financial Manager

CMA: Certified Management Accountant

CMC: Certified Management Consultant

CMFC: Chartered Mutual Fund Counselor

CMT: Chartered Market Technician

CPA: Certified Public Accountant

CPCU: Chartered Property Casualty Underwriter

CRPC: Chartered Retirement Planning Counselor

MBA: Master of Business Administration

PFS: Personal Financial Specialist

REBC: Registered Employee Benefits Consultant

RHU: Registered Health Underwriter

RIA: Registered Investment Advisor

RR: Registered Representative

Questions to Ask a Credit Counselor

If you have found yourself deep in debt and determine that you need a credit counselor, you will want to be sure that you have a good one and are not being scammed. Here are some good questions to ask to help you determine if the credit counselor is right for you.

1. What services do you offer?

2. Do you have any education materials I may look at and take home? Are they on the Internet?

3. Do you counsel about my current problems and suggest solutions to keep me out of financial trouble in the future?

4. What are your fees?

5. Are there any upfront fees before you help?

6. Are there monthly fees?

7. What do these fees provide me?

8. Who backs you or your organization?

9. Do you provide a contract?

10. Who oversees your organization?

11. What qualifications do you have?

12. Can you get my creditors to lower my interest rate, get rid of finance charges, and waive late fees?

13. Will my personal information be kept confidential?

Questions to Ask When Choosing a Real Estate Agent

1. What is your training and experience?

2. What do you know about the area in which I wish to live?

3. Based on what I have told you concerning my needs for a home, what type of home would you recommend? What do you know about homes such as this?

4. What is the biggest issue when dealing with a seller? How do you overcome that issue?

5. Do you have a list of recommendations for inspectors, title attorneys, surveyors, and other professionals?

6. Will you be helping me or will it be someone else?

7. If I have questions or concerns, will I be speaking to you personally?

8. Can you give me some references?

9. What fees are associated with working with you?

10. When are these fees paid?

Questions to Ask When Hiring a Stockbroker

1. What licenses to you hold?

2. What is your training and experience?

3. What is your investing philosophy? (You need to be sure that your broker's "picks" would be the kind of things you want to invest in. For instance, they may love small company stocks and you may feel uncomfortable with them. If this is true, then you will need to find a different stockbroker.)

4. How big is your firm?

5. Will you be doing all my work? If not, who will?

6. Will I be able to speak with you personally if I have problems or questions?

7. Who is your broker dealer?

8. Have you ever had any disciplinary actions taken against you? (You can always check your stockbroker by going to www.nasdr.com)

9. May I have some references?

10. What will you need from me and what will you provide?

11. How often will we interact?

12. How do you set your fees?

13. What are your billing policies?

Tax Time Records

1. Income records (including self-employed income)

*If you are self-employed and use your home as an office, you will need to have your mortgage payments, electric, phone, and other home expenses. See a CPA about these needs

2. Reports of stock purchases and sales

3. Statements sent to you by your brokerage company, mutual funds company, or any other investment company

4. Records of acquired securities

5. Dividends for dividend reinvestment plans

6. Records of IRA or other retirement fund contributions

7. Documentation for worthless securities

8. Interest expense documentation

9. Travel and meal expense documentation

10. Home improvement records

11. Home selling expenses

12. Charitable donation records

13. Records of stock given away

14. Records of tax help and legal counsel

GLOSSARY

401(K) PLAN — A qualified plan established by employers to which eligible employees may make salary-deferred (salary reduction) contributions on a post- and/or pre-tax basis. Employers may make matching or nonelective contributions to the plan on behalf of eligible employees and may also add a profit-sharing feature to the plan. Earnings accrue on a tax-deferred basis. A type of annuity contract that delays payments of income, installments or a lump sum until the investor elects to receive them. This type of annuity has two main phases, the savings phase in which you invest money into the account, and the income phase when payments are received. A deferred annuity can be either variable or fixed.

A

ACCOUNT AGREEMENT — An agreement which you sign and which lists your rights and responsibilities and the bank's rights and responsibilities for the bank account.

ACCOUNTS PAYABLE — Money owed by a business for goods and services received.

ACCOUNTS RECEIVABLE — Money owed to a business by purchasers of goods and/or services.

ACCUMULATION PERIOD 1 – Phase in an investor's life when he/she builds up savings and the value of an investment portfolio with the intention of having a nest egg for retirement.

ACTIVE-PARTICIPANT STATUS — Refers to an individual's participation in an employer sponsored retirement plan. The plans which qualify include:

1. Qualified plans, such as profit sharing plans, defined benefit plans, money purchase pension or target benefit plans and 401(k) plans

2. SEP IRAs

3. SIMPLE IRAs

4. 403(b) plans

5. Qualified annuity plans

6. Employee Funded Pension Trusts (created before June 25, 1959) A plan established for its employees by the United States, by a state or political subdivision of the United States, or by an agency or instrumentality of the United States or any of its subdivisions

ADJUSTABLE RATE MORTGAGE — A mortgage with an interest rate that is likely to change over the term of the loan. It is also dependent on influences such as interest rates on Treasury securities.

ADJUSTED BALANCE — A method of calculating your credit balance and annual percentage rate (APR) where payments and/or credits made during the billing cycle are subtracted from your balance at the end of the previous billing cycle. This method is more advantageous to borrowers and credit card holders. Unlike Average Daily Balance calculations, new purchases during that billing cycle are not included in adjusted balance calculations, and interest is only applied to the balance remaining after payments are credited to your account.

ADVERSE ACTION — Any negative action taken as a result of information contained in your consumer report.

AFFINITY CARD — A credit card that makes a donation to a charity of your choice based up on how much you spend. Chances are such a credit card has a higher interest rate than the standard.

AMORTIZATION – Amortization is a payment plan that allows the borrower to reduce his/her debt through monthly payments of principal. The process of fully paying off a debt by installments over a fixed time.

ANNUAL PERCENTAGE RATE (APR) — A measure of how much interest credit will cost a borrower. APR is the yearly rate lenders charge borrowers to borrow money (also called the cost of credit). Lenders must divulge the APR they are charging prior to finalizing the deal. Lenders cannot reveal or make changes to the APR after the lender/borrower contract has been signed. However, some credit card companies and loan companies state in their agreement that they can change your APR when interest rates or indexes change.

ANNUITANT — (1) A person who receives the benefits of an annuity or pension. (2) The person upon whom a life-insurance contract is based.

APPRAISAL — A judgment or estimate of the quality or value of real estate, made by a professional appraiser as of a given date.

ASSET — All money, investments, and property owned by an individual, family, or business.

ASSUMED INTEREST RATE (AIR) –Rate of interest or growth rate selected by an insurance company. The assumed interest rate is provided to determine the value of an annuity contract and, therefore, the periodic income payment which can be provided to the annuitant.

AUTOMATIC DEFERRAL DEFAULT PERCENTAGE — Percentage of pay that is deferred when an employee is enrolled in a plan through its automatic enrollment feature. The typical automatic deferral default percentage is 3 percent of pay. Participants can generally choose to defer an amount other than the default percentage.

AUTOMATIC ROLLOVER — A rollover of a participant's qualified plan balance to an IRA without the participant's authorization.

AUTOMATIC STAY — A stay imposed by the court when a bankruptcy is filed that prevents creditors from taking collection actions against the debtor.

AVERAGE DAILY BALANCE – A method of calculation of your credit balance and interest; the practice of crediting your account from the day your payment is received; a daily tracking of what you owe. When calculating the average daily balance, the lender adds the beginning balance for each day in the billing period and then subtracts any payments and/or credits made to your account that day. The result is your average daily balance. New purchases are not necessarily added to your account the day of the purchase and will not show in your daily balance. When the purchase is charged to your account, it affects your balance.

B

BACK-END LOAD — A fee paid by the investor when he or she sells a mutual fund within a certain time period.

BALANCED FUND — A mutual fund that invests in a mix of stocks and bonds. The fund manager determines which stocks and bonds to invest in and at what proportions.

BALLOON LOAN — A short-term fixed rate loan involving lower payments for a set period of time, ending with one large payment for the remaining amount of the principal at a time specified in the contract.

BANKRUPTCY — A proceeding in U.S. Bankruptcy Court that

may legally release a person from repaying debts owed. Credit reports normally include bankruptcies for up to 10 years. It is a form of financial protection where the borrower is unable to pay rent or mortgage payments, has no credit or means of paying for it, and is unable to reconcile with collection agencies. There are two methods of filing for personal bankruptcy: Chapter 7 and Chapter 13. A Chapter 7 bankruptcy eliminates all debts (minus taxes and possibly alimony payments) by taking all non-exempt property (as set forth in Chapter 7 filing) and converting it to cash to pay off debts. A Chapter 13 bankruptcy allows a borrower with a steady income to pay off bills over a 36-to 60-month period. Chapter 13 filing is only available to those who have predictable income and a means of paying off their debt over the established period of time.

BENEFICIARY — A person or entity named in a will or a financial contract as the inheritor of property when the property owner dies.

BONDS — Offered by governments and corporations, bonds are investments in which you lend a sum of money to the issuer for a set amount of time at a fixed rate of interest.

BOOMERANG — An American slang term that refers to an adult who has moved back in with his or her parents (who are part of the baby boom generation) instead of living independently. The phrase, when applied to an individual, refers to a person who has lived independently for a time before returning home due to the financial costs associated with maintaining a separate household.

BULL AND BEAR MARKETS — When stock prices are increasing in a healthy market, it is a bull market. When stock prices are decreasing, it is a bear market.

C

CAFETERIA PLAN — An employee benefit plan that allows staff to choose from a variety of benefits to formulate a plan that best suits their needs. Also known as "cafeteria employee benefit plan" or "flexible benefit plan."

CAPITAL GAINS TREATMENT — Specific taxes assessed on investment capital gains as determined by the U.S.

Tax Code. When a stock is sold for a profit, the portion of the proceeds over and above the purchase value (or cost basis) is known as capital gains. Capital gains tax is broken down into two categories: short-term capital gains and long-term capital gains. Stocks held longer than one year are considered long-term for the treatment of any capital gains, and are taxed a maximum of 15 percent depending on the investor's tax bracket. Stocks held less than one year are subject to short-term capital gains at a maximum rate of 35 percent depending again on the investor's tax bracket.

CAPITAL GROWTH STRATEGY – An asset allocation strategy that seeks to maximize capital appreciation or the increase in value of a portfolio or asset over the long term.

CASH OR DEFERRED ARRANGEMENT (CODA) — A type of profit sharing or stock bonus plan in which employees may defer current pre-tax compensation.

CERTIFICATE OF DEPOSIT — A certificate of deposit is made with a bank, credit union, or savings and loan. The deposit is a specified amount for a certain period and a set interest rate. There are no fees on CDs, but a penalty is charged for early withdrawal.

CHARGE-OFF — The balance on a credit obligation that a lender no longer expects to be repaid and writes off as a bad debt.

CHARITABLE LEAD TRUST — A trust designed to reduce beneficiaries' taxable income by first donating a portion of the trust's income to charities and then, after a specified period of time, transferring the remainder of the trust to the beneficiaries.

CLIFF VESTING — A type of vesting that occurs entirely at a specified time rather than gradually.

CLOSING COSTS — Any costs other than interest added to the loan, which can include any appraiser fees, points paid, or other miscellaneous fees.

COLLECTION — Attempted recovery of a past-due credit obligation by a collection department or agency.

COMPOUNDING — Refers to earning income on your income. For example, on fixed income investments that pay interest over time at periodic intervals, compounding means making interest on your initial investment and also on the interest as it builds up.

CONSOLIDATED OMNIBUS BUDGET RECONCILIATION ACT (COBRA) — A health plan that states that if you leave your job for any reason and were an active participant in the company's health plan prior to your departure date, you have the right, if you wish, to continue the health insurance coverage you and your family received for 18 months at your own cost.

CONSUMER CREDIT FILE — A credit bureau record on a given individual. It may include consumer name, address, social security number, credit history, inquiries, collection records, and public records such as bankruptcy filings and tax liens.

CONSUMER FINANCE — Refers to any kind of lending to consumers. However, in the United States financial services industry, the term "consumer finance" often refers to a particular type of business, sub prime branch lending (that is lending to people with less than perfect credit). Examples of these companies include HSBC Finance, CIT, Citifinancial, and Wells Fargo Financial.

COVERDELL EDUCATION SAVINGS ACCOUNT (ESA) — A tax-deferred account created by the U.S. government to assist families in funding educational expenses.

CREDIT BUREAU — A credit reporting agency that is a clearinghouse for information on the credit rating of individuals or firms is often called a "credit repository" or a "consumer reporting agency." The three largest credit bureaus in the United States are Equifax, Experian, and TransUnion.

CREDIT BUREAU RISK SCORE — A type of credit score based solely on data stored at the major credit bureaus. It offers a snapshot of a consumer's credit risk at a particular point and rates the likelihood that the consumer will repay debts as agreed.

CREDIT OPPORTUNITY ACT (ECOA) — Federal legislation that prohibits discrimination in credit. The ECOA originally was enacted in 1974 as Title VII of the Consumer Credit Protection Act. It ensures that all consumers are given an equal chance to obtain credit and that such factors as race, national origin, gender, or religion are not used to deny credit to those who would be otherwise eligible.

CREDIT SCORE — Term used for credit bureau risk scores. It broadly refers to a number generated by a statistical model used to evaluate information in making a credit decision. It is a statistical calculation of the credit information obtained in a consumer's credit report and is used to calculate your historical credit history.

CREDIT UNION — A nonprofit, cooperative financial institution owned and run by its members. Members pool their funds to make loans to each other. The volunteer board that runs each credit union is elected by the members. Most credit unions are organized to serve people in a particular community, group or groups of employees, or members of an organization or association.

CUSTODIAL ACCOUNT – (1) An account created at a bank, brokerage firm, or mutual fund company that is managed by an adult for a minor that is under the age of 18 to 21 (depending on state legislation). (2) A retirement account managed for eligible employees by a custodian.

DEBIT – Another name for withdrawal of funds from your account.

DEBIT CARD – Another name for a bank card that allows you to access your deposit accounts electronically. You can use it at banking machines or to pay for purchases at retailers using the direct payment service.

D

DEBT LOAD – Total amount of money the consumer owes.

DEBT-TO-INCOME RATIO – A comparison of gross income to housing and non-housing expenses; with the FHA, the-monthly mortgage payment should be no more than 29 percent of monthly gross income (before taxes) and the mortgage payment combined with non-housing debts should not exceed 41 percent of income.

DEFINED-BENEFIT PLAN – An employer-sponsored retirement plan where employee benefits are sorted out based on a formula, using factors such as salary history and duration of employment. Investment risk and portfolio management are entirely under the control of the company. There are also restrictions on when and how you can withdraw these funds without penalties. Also referred to as a "qualified benefit plan" or "non-qualified benefit plan."

DEFINED-CONTRIBUTION PLAN – A retirement plan in which a certain amount or percentage of money is set aside each year by a company for the benefit of the employee. There are restrictions as to when and how you can withdraw these funds without penalties.

DEFLATION – An actual decline in the general level of prices in the economy.

DEMAND LOAN – A loan that must be repaid in full on demand.

DIRECT DEPOSIT – A regular payment made directly into your account, usually from an employer.

DIRECT ROLLOVER – A distribution of eligible rollover assets from a qualified plan, 403(b) plan, or a governmental 457 plan to a Traditional IRA, qualified plan, 403(b) plan, or a governmental 457 plan; or a distribution from an IRA to a qualified plan, 403(b) plan or a governmental 457 plan, usually done to avoid taxes.

DISCRIMINATION TESTING – Tax qualified retirement plans must be administered in compliance with several regulations requiring numerical measurements. Typically, the process of determining whether the plan is in compliance is collectively called discrimination testing.

DIVERSIFICATION – Strives to smooth out unsystematic risk events in a portfolio so that the positive performance of some investments will neutralize the negative performance of others. Therefore, the benefits of diversification will hold only if the securities in the portfolio are not perfectly correlated.

DIVIDENDS – Company earnings paid out to shareholders according to the number of shares or stocks they hold. Dividends can be earned on stocks and certain mutual funds.

DOWN PAYMENT – Available cash after closing costs to be paid up front rather than financed.

E

EARLY WITHDRAWAL – Removal of funds from a fixed-term investment before the maturity date, or the removal of funds from a tax-deferred investment account or retirement savings account (such as an IRA) before a prescribed time, such as the account owner's attainment of a minimum age requirement.

EARNED INCOME –Payment you receive from your work or job. Salary, wages, self-employment income, alimony, and farming income are examples of earned income. Interest, dividends, social security payments, and pension payments are examples of unearned income.

ECONOMIC GROWTH AND TAX RELIEF RECONCILIATION ACT OF 2001 – EGTRRA – A U.S. tax law, effective for tax years beginning in 2002, that made some of the most important changes to retirement plans, including increasing contributions and deductibility limits for IRA and employer-sponsored plans and expanding portability rules for retirement plans in general. EGTRRA also increased the estate-tax exclusion and increased the generation-skipping transfer-tax exemption amounts.

EMPLOYEE CONTRIBUTION PLAN – A company-sponsored retirement plan to which employees make deposits (contributions) to an account. Contributions are deducted from employee's pay; some companies match those payments.

ENDORSE – To sign the back of a check to be able to cash it.

EQUITY – The difference between the price for which a property could be sold and the total debts registered against it.

ESCROW – Property or money held by a third party until the agreed upon obligations of a contract are met.

F

FACTS AND CIRCUMSTANCES TEST – determines whether financial need exists for a 401(k) hardship withdrawal.

FAIR CREDIT REPORTING ACT (FCRA) – Federal legislation that promotes the accuracy, confidentiality, and proper use of information in the files of every "consumer reporting agency." It was enacted in 1970.

FAIR DEBT COLLECTION PRACTICES ACT (FDCPA) – A federal law prohibiting abusive and unfair debt collection practices.

FICO® SCORES – Credit bureau risk scores produced from models developed by Fair Isaac Corporation are commonly known as FICO scores. Fair Isaac credit bureau scores are used by lenders and others to assess the credit risk of prospective borrowers or existing customers to help make credit and marketing decisions. These scores are derived solely from the information available on credit bureau reports. It is a mathematical equation/calculation lenders use to evaluate the risk associated with lending your money.

FIXED RATE — An annual percentage interest rate that does not change during the term of the loan.

FORECLOSURE - Foreclosure refers to the lender's legal action to take possession of the property (such as a house) used to secure repayment for a loan when a debtor fails to meet his obligations to pay back a loan.

H

HOME EQUITY LINE OF CREDIT (HELOC) — A mortgage loan that allows the borrower to obtain multiple advances of the loan proceeds at his or her discretion, up to an amount that represents a specified percentage of the borrower's equity in property.

I

INDIVIDUAL RETIREMENT ACCOUNT (IRA) - An IRA is a retirement investing tool that can be either an "individual retirement account" or an "individual retirement annuity." There are several types of IRAs: traditional IRAs, Roth IRAs, simple IRAs and SEP IRAs. Traditional and Roth IRAs are established by individual taxpayers, who are allowed to contribute 100 percent of compensation (self-employment income for sole proprietors and partners) up to a set maximum dollar amount. Contributions to the traditional IRA may be tax-deductible depending on the taxpayer's income, tax-filing status, and coverage by an employer-sponsored retirement plan. Roth IRA contributions are not tax-deductible.

INHERITANCE TAX — In some states a tax imposed on those who inherit assets from a deceased person. The tax rate for inheritance taxes depends on the value of the property received by the heir or beneficiary and his/her relationship to the decedent. Inheritance tax is known in some countries as a "death duty" and is occasionally called "the last twist of the taxman's knife."

INQUIRY — An item on a consumer's credit report that

shows that someone with a "permissible purpose" (under FCRA rules) has previously requested a copy of the consumer's report. Fair Isaac credit bureau risk scores take into account only inquiries resulting from a consumer's application for credit.

INSTALLMENT CREDIT — Loan repaid with interest owed in equal periodic payments of principal and interest. Installment loans are fully amortizing loans, repayable over a fixed amortization schedule in monthly installments. These loans can be secured by personal property, for example, an auto loan, but not real estate. If the loan is to a consumer, disclosure of finance charges is required by federal consumer protection laws.

INTEREST — A percentage charged to the remaining amount owed when you borrow money, assuming that there are no prepayments of principal.

INTESTACY — Act of dying without a legal will.

INVESTMENT CONSULTANT – An advisor who helps investors with their long-term investment planning. An investment consultant, unlike a broker, does more in-depth work on formulating clients' investment strategies, helping them fulfill their needs and goals.

IRA ADOPTION AGREEMENT AND PLAN DOCUMENT — A contract between the IRA holder and the financial institution. It explains the provisions of the IRA.

K

KEOGH PLAN — A defined-benefit plan or defined-contribution plan established by self-employed persons and their employees.

L

LENDER — A person or company that offers to loan money to a borrower for a given period of time. The borrower is obliged to repay the loan according to the agreed upon terms and with specified interest.

LINE OF CREDIT — An agreement negotiated between a borrower and a lender establishing the maximum amount of money a borrower may draw. The agreement also sets out other conditions, such as how and when money is to be repaid.

LUMP-SUM DISTRIBUTION — A one-time payment for the entire amount due, rather than breaking payments into smaller installments.

M

MACROECONOMICS — Looking at the economy as a whole, particularly the interaction of its various components with one another.

MARITAL PROPERTY — A U.S. state-level legal distinction of a married individual's assets. Property acquired by either spouse during the course of a marriage is considered marital property. For example, an IRA in the name of an individual with a spouse, which is accumulated during the course of the marriage, would be considered marital property.

MATCHING CONTRIBUTION — A type of contribution an employer chooses to make to an employee's employer-sponsored retirement plan. The contribution is based on elective deferral contributions made by the employee.

MATCHING STRATEGY — A means of creating investment portfolios that meet the individual needs of investors through tiered investment durations.

MICROECONOMICS — Looking at the individual parts of the economy with emphasis on the market process.

MORTGAGE BROKERS — Trained professionals who seek the best loan rates for borrowers, working as a connection between banks and borrowers.

MUTUAL FUND — An investment product in which your money is pooled with the money of many other investors.

N

NATIONAL FOUNDATION FOR CONSUMER CREDIT — A nonprofit organization that educates consumers about using credit wisely. The NFCC is the parent group for Consumer Credit Counseling Service.

NON SUFFICIENT FUNDS (NSF) — If a check is returned for

this reason, it means that there was not enough money in your bank account to cover the amount of the check. There is a fee to you if this situation occurs.

NON-DISCHARGEABLE DEBT — A debt that cannot be eliminated in bankruptcy proceedings.

NONELECTIVE CONTRIBUTION — A type of contribution an employer chooses to make to each of his or her eligible employee's employer-sponsored retirement plan. The contribution is not based on salary reduction contributions made by the employee.

P

PAID AS AGREED — A designation on the credit report that indicates the consumer is repaying the credit account according to the terms of the credit agreement.

PASSBOOK — A book in which all the transactions in a bank account are noted. This book may list the transaction codes and the customer's responsibilities.

PENSION FUND — A fund established by an employer to facilitate and organize the investment of employees' retirement funds contributed by the employer and employees. The pension fund is a common asset pool meant to generate stable growth over the long term, and provide pensions for employees when they reach the end of their working years and commence retirement.

PENSION PLAN — A retirement plan, usually tax exempt, wherein the employer makes contributions for the employee. Many pension plans are being replaced by the 401(k).

PENSION SHORTFALL — A situation in which a company offering employees a defined benefit plan does not have enough money set aside to meet the pension obligations to employees who will be retired in the future.

PERSONAL FINANCE GLOSSARY

PERSONAL IDENTIFICATION NUMBER (PIN) — A unique number or pass code entered by a customer when using an Automated Teller that gives the customer access to his or her account.

PMI PAYMENT, PRIVATE MORTGAGE INSURANCE

(PMI) — For home loans secured with less than 20 percent down, PMI is commonly added to insure the bank you are borrowing money from. PMI occurs until you build up enough equity to exceed 20 percent of the original purchase price, at which time you must request that your PMI be removed from your loan.

POINTS — Total units of prepaid interest used to reduce the interest rate of your mortgage. Each point equals 1 percent of your mortgage balance.

PRINCIPAL — Amount still owed on a loan, excluding interest.

R

RATE CAP — Maximum amount that the interest rate on an adjustable rate mortgage loan can rise in a single year.

RE-AGE — When an account status is updated to reflect "current" when the account is delinquent.

REAL ESTATE AGENT — A person trained and licensed to deal with the purchase, sale, and marketing of real estate property.

RECONCILIATION — Checking all bank account papers to make sure that the bank's records and your records agree.

REFINANCING — To replace an existing mortgage with a new mortgage on the same property, typically at a lower rate.

REVERSE MORTGAGE — A special type of loan used to convert the equity in a home into cash. The money obtained through a reverse mortgage is usually used to provide seniors with financial security in their retirement years.

REVOKED IRA — An IRA holder may revoke an IRA within the seven days after it is established. When an IRA holder elects to revoke the IRA, the full amount contributed to the IRA must be returned to the IRA holder.

ROLLOVER — (1) Process of reinvesting funds from a mature security into a new issue of the same or a similar security. (2) Process of transferring the holdings of one retirement plan to another without suffering tax consequences. (3). Charge that is incurred by Forex investors who rollover their positions to the following delivery date.

ROTH 401(K) — A new employer-sponsored investment savings account that is funded with after-tax money. After investor reaches age 59.5, withdrawals of any money from the account (including investment gains) are tax-free. Unlike the Roth IRA, the Roth 401(k) has no income limitations for those investors who want to participate — anyone, no matter what his/her income, is allowed to invest up to the contribution limit into the plan.

ROTH IRA — An individual retirement plan that bears many similarities to the Traditional IRA. Contributions are never deductible, and qualified distributions are tax-free.

S

SERVICE CHARGE — A fee paid for using a service.

T

TAX-SHELTERED — A tax shelter is a savings or investment plan that offers tax savings.

TERM — Length of time you have to pay back a loan.

TOTAL CLOSING COSTS — Amount of up front costs paid before your loan can be issued, such as a loan origination fee and any points.

TREASURY BILLS (T-BILLS) — Short-term government obligations that are payable to the bearer and sold on a discount basis; the difference between a T-bill's market or discounted price and its face or redemption value is effectively interest if the T-bill is held to maturity.

U

UNIFIED MANAGED ACCOUNT (UMA) – A professionally managed private investment account that is rebalanced regularly and can encompass every investment vehicle (e.g., mutual funds, stocks, bonds and exchange traded funds) in an investor's portfolio, all in a single account.

W

WITHDRAWAL — Money taken out of an account. The withdrawal may be in cash, by check, debit card, or by automatic withdrawal.

Index